CORNWALL LIBRARY

G000255899

LIS
ST AUS
23/12/19

WITHDRAWN

Tale

24 HOUR RENEWAL HOTLINE 0845 607 6119

www.cornwall.gov.uk/library

one and all    onen hag oll

# Plymouth
# Tales from the Past
by
Derek Tait

Driftwood Coast Publishing

Frontispiece : A girl helps the War Effort by collecting milk bottle tops.

First published 2010

Driftwood Coast Publishing
PO Box 7,West Park,Plymouth,PL5 2YS.
© Derek Tait, 2010

The right of Derek Tait to be identified as the Author
of this work has been asserted in accordance with the
Copyrights, Designs and Patents Act 1988.

All rights reserved. No part of this book may be reprinted
or reproduced or utilised in any form or by any electronic,
mechanical or other means, now known or hereafter invented,
including photocopying and recording, or in any storage or retrieval
system, without the permission in writing from the publishers.

| CORNWALL COUNTY LIBRARY | | |
|---|---|---|
| 38009046481013 | | |
| **Bertrams** | 26/08/2010 | |
| AN | £9.99 | TAIT DEREK Plymouth 679252/00029 - 1 of 4 |
| LIS | | |

# Contents

# Acknowledgements

Photo credits: Barry Ewart, The BBC, Derek Tait, Evening Herald, Kim Precious, Marshall Ware, Maurice Dart, The Driftwood Coast Photo Library, Steve Johnson, Western Morning News. I have tried to track down the copyright holders of all photos used and apologise to anyone who hasn't been mentioned.

## Books:
Plymouth, Plymouth at War, Saltash Passage, Plymouth Hoe, Mount Edgcumbe by Derek Tait (Driftwood Coast Publishing).
Plymouth : Pictures from the Past by Guy Fleming (Devon Books).
Plymouth and Plymothians (Winram Cluer).

## Websites:
Brian Moseley's Plymouth Data website at: www.plymouthdata.info

## Newspapers
Evening Herald, Western Morning News.

Driftwood Coast Publishing
© Derek Tait 2010

# Introduction

I'm always pleased to hear from people who have enjoyed reading my books. For quite a while now, I have been writing a local history blog on the internet and sections of the blog are regularly featured in The Herald. I know that there are still many people who aren't on the internet and some people have even said to me, 'What's a blog?'. For all those people, and for all the people who would rather enjoy reading and holding a book (like myself), I've compiled this collection of my favourite stories from Plymouth's past which I hope you'll find both interesting and informative.

Stories include items about the Civil War battle at St Budeaux, the Romans, Harry Houdini, Buffalo Bill, Laurel and Hardy and even Benny Hill. More recent history includes tales about the much loved Plymouth Zoo, Westward Television and the visit to the Westcountry by the Beatles.

Plymouth is linked with many influential figures from the past and some are mentioned within these pages including Charles Darwin, Scott of the Antarctic, Mary Newman, Lawrence of Arabia, Sir Arthur Conan Doyle, Fletcher Christian and many others.

Some of the stories featured within these pages I'm sure that you will be familiar with, like Houdini's jump from the Stonehouse Bridge in 1909, but I hope that many will be new to you.

Some people will remember actual events mentioned within the book or remember their parents or grandparents talking about past events. Many older people living in Plymouth will have knowledge passed down to them from their recent ancestors telling of the time when Buffalo Bill came to Plymouth or when Red Indians were to be found in Union Street. Many people will also have memories of dancing on the Pier or dancing on the Hoe during the War years. Others will remember the city as it once was before the Blitz of 1941.

There are many plaques around the city celebrating adventurers, explorers, heroic figures and writers but many of these seem to go unnoticed and I hope the tales included here will give some insight to the people behind the names. I'm sure that many people will have seen the lines from Arthur Conan Doyle's Sherlock Holmes books embedded in the pavements at Durnford Street in Stonehouse.

If you are connected to the internet and want to keep up to date with my blog, then please go to http://plymouthlocalhistory.blogspot.com/ for more stories of Plymouth's past. I hope that you find the tales within this book both informative and enjoyable.

# Higher St Budeaux
# and the Civil War

I was driving by Higher St Budeaux Church recently when I noticed the piece of land that was being cleared nearby. I'm sure that many people will know that when the road was widened in 1910, musket and cannon balls from the Civil War were found there and some are kept at the city's museum. Marshall Ware wrote a very interesting piece about the battle, entitled 'When Cromwell zapped St Budeaux', in the Evening Herald back in the 1980s. I'm sure that there will be many historical artefacts to be found but I don't know if there will be any sort of investigation. For anyone interested in the church and the Civil War, there is more mentioned in my book about St Budeaux.

Plymouth and its surrounding villages such as St Budeaux had sworn an oath to fight and die for the Parliamentarian cause. Those who did not comply faced hanging. However, in Cornwall, the people supported the Royalist cause and made raids across the water on parts of St Budeaux. For a time, the church at Higher St Budeaux was used as a garrison by the Royalists. On 16th April 1644, Lieutenant Colonel Martin, who commanded the Parliamentarian garrison at Plymouth, sent 600 musketeers, with 120 horses, to attack the 500 Cavaliers stationed at St Budeaux. Because of a mistake made by guides, the horses went one way and the attacking party went another way. Nevertheless, the foot soldiers arrived at the church, and not being expected, saw off the enemy and captured the church tower. Altogether, they captured 2 officers and 44 other prisoners. They also took three barrels of gunpowder, 20 horses and about 20 arms. It was said that most of the prisoners then joined the Parliament forces and who could blame them when you consider the alternative.

On the 27th December 1644, St Budeaux was again the scene of much bloodshed. From Kinterbury, the Roundheads marched towards the church, which was now a garrison for the Parliamentarians, and fought for an hour and a half before the church was recaptured. The Royalists also captured a Major Stucley together with 20 officers and 100 soldiers. Ten of the defenders were killed as were seven of the Roundheads including a Major Haynes. A mound in a garden at Plaistow Hill, near the church, is said to be the place where those who died in the battle were buried.

During the siege of Plymouth by the Royalists, the inhabitants of St Budeaux would take provisions into town for the men and their horses. Prince Maurice issued a warrant which stated, 'To the constables or tythingmen of Saint Budeaux and Pennyross, threatening proceedings against all who should carry with him horse, oxen or kine, or sheep or other provision for men or horse into the said town of Plymouth for the relief of the rebells there.'

After the battle, the church was little more than a wreck and it wasn't restored until 1655.

# Plymouth Zoo

I'm sure that many people will have fond memories of Plymouth Zoo. I remember going there in the late 1960s and a pelican called Percy following us around. It was a lovely place to start off with but got a bit run down and smelly towards the end. Amazingly, the zoo was only open for 16 years. It opened on Thursday April 19th 1962 at a cost of £30,000 and it had 13,000 visitors during the first three days.

The zoo was owned by the Chipperfields and was a very popular attraction. It had many animals including chimpanzees, polar bears, seals, camels, giraffes and lions etc. There's a great movie at the Pathe News site and all the animals look very happy. I know the keepers were very interested in their welfare and got quite attached to the animals. When you're a child, a zoo seems a wondrous place but when you're older and with hindsight, it seems unfair keeping them all cooped up in cages. I remember the chimpanzees at the beginning of the zoo would collect up gravel and throw it at the visitors! There was an article about a chimp in the news in a Swedish Zoo recently doing exactly the same thing and it was reported as if it was something new.

Percy the Pelican who seemed to wander free throughout the zoo hoping for food from visitors. He was certainly fed a lot of stale bread by local children!

The elephant was one of my favourites, I think that she might have been called Nellie. I only remember one elephant but I'm sure the zoo had others during the time it was open.

I remember the sweet popcorn that was sold at the cafe to feed the animals. All the children always ended up eating it themselves although I'm sure it wouldn't have done the animals much good anyway. I remember there was a giraffe that was about to swallow a popcorn packet. Luckily, the keeper managed to get it off him before he choked! There was a children's area with guinea pigs and rabbits and a huge tortoise which I believe was a gift from the Navy in the early 1960s. The zoo closed on Sunday January 8th 1978 and was later converted into a skateboard park. Now, it seems to have been incorporated into Argyle's new stadium.

We certainly had some good times there and I miss it but I think with concerns over animal welfare, I'm quite glad that it's no longer there.

# The Blue Monkey

Although the public house has now been knocked down, the area near to the Higher St Budeaux Church will probably always be known as the Blue Monkey. It had previously been called Church Inn, St Bude Inn, St Budeaux Inn and Ye Old St Budeaux Inn before becoming the Blue Monkey. The owner of the Church Inn was a Lord Graves who owned the Barton of Ernesettle in 1798. He was also Lord of the Manor of Agaton. Frances Martin is recorded as being the landlord of the pub in 1823. He was responsible for changing the pub's name to the St Bude Inn, in 1828. In 1862, the War Department bought the then named St Budeaux Inn. In 1914, the Secretary of State for the Department sold the premises, which included a stables, to James Alger for £1,050. Alger changed the name of the pub to Ye Old St Budeaux Inn on 4 May 1937. He later changed the name again to The Blue Monkey early in 1939 and later sold the Inn to the Octagon Brewery in December 1939 for £12,750.

A newspaper cutting that used to hang in the bar said that a Mr Dunsford, the then landlord, changed the name to the Blue Monkey when the Stafford Regiment was stationed at Devonport. However, the deeds say that the name was changed in 1939 by James Algar. The reason, according to locals, was that Algar had seen a monkey which had escaped from a shed at Agaton on the roof of the Inn.

Apparently, the change of name and the swinging monkey sign wasn't popular, even though it's the one best remembered, so it was replaced by a square sign , featuring a Naval Blue Monkey Boy, in honour of the boys who packed the guns with powder during the Battle of Trafalgar in 1805. They were known as powder monkeys and the job left them with blue residue on their hands and this has also been taken as the origin of the pub's name, The Blue Monkey. Perhaps both stories are true and it would be interesting to think that a monkey once ran around on the roof of the Inn.

Incidentally, before the sign change, in the early 1980s, I was walking by the Inn and there was the swinging monkey sign, slightly battered and put out for the dustbin men to collect. I wish I'd picked it up and kept it as a souvenir now! I was recently told that the sign turned up at the Stacks Reclamation yard nearby, some years later. I never saw it but I hope that someone has it in their collection somewhere.

In its final years, the Inn developed a bad reputation and finally closed and was eventually bricked up. It was for sale for many years before an arson attack destroyed the inside and the roof. From then on, its days were numbered and early in March 2007, it was unfortunately demolished. The post where the Blue Monkey sign once hung is still there and recently, someone has repainted the words, 'Blue Monkey' at the top. Perhaps the council were responsible for this as, although the pub is long gone, the area will forever be known as the Blue Monkey. I'm sure in many years to come, people will wonder where such a comical name came from and I hope to produce a book of Place Names of Plymouth at some future date which maybe will reveal all to future generations.

# Harry Houdini

Harry Houdini appeared at the Palace Theatre of Varieties during August 1909. There was much excitement at his appearance and he challenged five joiners and mechanics at Devonport Dockyard to make a box from which he wouldn't be able to escape. They produced the box and Houdini was nailed inside. It took him twelve minutes to get out. Another of his daring feats involved him being securely handcuffed and diving from Halfpenny Bridge at Stonehouse.

The story was covered in the next day's Western Morning News:

**Western Morning News,**
**Wednesday August 18th 1909.**
**"The Handcuff King"**
**An Exciting Performance.**
**Harry Houdini, the "Handcuff King" who was performing at the Palace Theatre of Varieties, Plymouth this week gave a remarkable exhibition of his skill yesterday afternoon at Stonehouse. The intrepid performer had previously announced his intention of diving from the Halfpenny Gate Bridge, securely handcuffed, and this caused a huge crowd to assemble on the bridge itself and on the adjoining quays and banks.**
**Prompt to time Houdini appeared, stripped and poised himself on the parapet of the bridge. He was then handcuffed with his hands behind his back, while elbow locks were also worn, the chain passing around the neck. This accomplished, he immediately dived into the stream and disappeared from sight. Easily within the minute, the "Handcuff King" reappeared on the surface, carrying his fetters aloft in his right hand, while the crowd heartily cheered his exploit. Subsequently, Houdini said that he had performed the diving trick over fifty times. He was capable of staying under water well over three minutes, but should he not appear in three minutes there were always ready two or three assistants who would swim to his rescue. The handcuffs and chains weighed 18lb.**

What an amazing sight it must have been to see Houdini leap off Stonehouse Bridge or to see him performing at the Palace Theatre. There doesn't seem to be many photos, if any, of Houdini appearing in Plymouth and this seems quite strange as he would have been a huge celebrity at the time drawing huge crowds to his shows and outdoor stunts. He would have been very highly paid at the time and was known for his generosity to local charities and orphanages. It's hard to imagine what it would have been like in 1909 but the theatre would have had a great appeal and entertainment would have all been 'live' in a time when there were no televisions or cinemas. It's hard to imagine this world of the Edwardian period where all entertainment was either outdoors at concerts or in theatres. In an age where we are daily bombarded with entertainment in the form of television, cinema and the internet etc, shows like the ones given by Houdini and Buffalo Bill seem a world away from the entertainment of today.

# Execution on Plymouth Hoe

Between the Naval Memorial and the Hoe Lodge Gardens, there is a cross with the number '3' embedded in the pavement. This marks the spot where three Royal Marines were executed by firing squad on 6 July, 1797. Their names were Lee, Coffy and Branning and they were found guilty of attempting to excite a mutiny at Stonehouse Barracks. Another Marine, M Gennis was convicted of a similar crime and sentenced to 1000 lashes and transported to Botany Bay for life.

The incident was reported in the Sherborne and Yeovil Mercury on Monday 10th July,1797. It reads:

'PLYMOUTH, July 8 - On Wednesday morning an express arrived here from the War-Office, with a warrant for the execution of Lee, Coffy, and Branning, three marines who were last week tried by a General Court-Martial, and found guilty of an attempt to excite a mutiny among the marine corps at Stone-house Barracks and on Thursday at 12 o'clock the troops at this place and in the neighbourhood, consisting of the Sussex fencible cavalry, four companies of the royal artillery, the Lancashire, East Devon and Essex regiments of militia, the 25th regiment of foot, royal independent invalids, and Plymouth volunteers, assembled on the Hoe, and formed in a half circle in order to witness the execution. M Gennis, another marine tried for a similar crime, and sentenced to receive 1000 lashes, and to be afterwards transported to Botany Bay for life, was brought on the ground soon after twelve o'clock, and received 500 lashes, and then conveyed back to Stone-house Barracks. At half past one o'clock, Lee, Coffy and Branning were marched from the Citadel under the escort of a party of marines, with a coffin before each, preceded by the band of that corps playing the Dead March in Saul.

The former was attended by the Rev. Dr. Hawker; and the two latter by a Roman Catholic priest, who after praying with them near an hour, quitted them, and they all three knelt on their coffins for a few minutes, when an officer of marines came and drew the caps over their faces, and a party of twenty marines immediately came down and put a period to their existence by discharging the contents of their muskets through their bodies, after which all the regiments marched round them in solemn procession, the whole forming, perhaps, one of the most awful scenes that the human eye ever witnessed. They all behaved in a manner becoming their melancholy situation, and apparently very resigned and penitent. About thirty thousand people were supposed to be present at the execution'.

There was more to the execution than mentioned in the newspaper though. Ten thousand men of the Fleet and garrison were there to watch them die and most of Plymouth appeared to have turned out too. When the three men faced the firing squad and the shots were fired, Coffy and Branning fell forward, dead, into their coffins. However, Lee was not hit and had to go through the whole procedure again. The reserve firing squad lined up, took aim and fired but again Lee was untouched. Once more, they loaded up, took aim but again missed Lee. In the end, a Sergeant came up behind him and shot him dead at close range. It seems odd that the firing squad missed Lee three times and perhaps there was some sympathy with him amongst the troops.

Earlier fourteen seamen had been hanged at the yardarm on their ships in the Sound.

This was to be Plymouth's last public execution.

# Buffalo Bill's visit in 1904

Buffalo Bill visited the city on 3rd June, 1904.
The event was covered in the local newspaper:
**'Buffalo Bill's Visit To Plymouth.**
**3rd June, 1904.**
**Today Colonel WF Cody, known the world over as Buffalo Bill, gives
two performances at Plymouth today in the course of his final tour
of Great Britain with his unique exhibition of life in the Wild West.
The location of the show at the Exhibition Fields,**

**Pennycomequick, will make it readily accessible to residents of
Plymouth, Devonport and Stonehouse, and special arrangements
are being made by the railway companies to enable residents in**

outlying districts to witness the performance. No fewer than 800 horses participate in the show, and three special trains are employed to convey them and their properties from place to place. They arrived at Plymouth early this morning, and unloading, which occupied about two hours, began at 5.30. This show was patronised by thousands of people yesterday, on the occasion of its first visit to Bodmin. By the addition of a number of genuine Japanese soldiers to his Wild West, Colonel Cody has acted only in response to a great public desire to see and learn something of these remarkable little men. Another new feature introduced is a daring leap through space by a cowboy on a bicycle. This rider starts from a height of 95 feet, and riding swiftly down an incline jumps from the incline across 40 feet of space to a continuing platform, and thence out of the arena. It is a most daring feat. The really big feature among the new things introduced by the colonel for his season, however is 'Custer's Last Stand' or 'The Battle of Little Big Horn'. In this, over 300 men and horses participate, giving the most realistic representation of differing methods of warfare pursued by white and red man ever attempted, and making faithful representation of the massacre of Custer and 300 members of his regiment by a band of over 7,000 Indians led by the famous old chieftain Sitting Bull, whose only son, Willie Sitting Bull is now a member of Colonel Cody's company, and is a daily participant in the mock battle. For the benefit of the country visitors, the Great Western Railway will run a late special train, which will leave Millbay at 10.55 pm calling at North-Road and Mutley for Plymstock, Billacombe, Elburton Cross, Brixton Road, Steer Point and Yealmpton.'

It must have been amazing to have been a child in 1904 and to have been taken to see Buffalo Bill's Wild West Show. Imagine their delight at seeing a real character from the Wild West complete with many Red Indians taking part in mock battles. America would have seemed a world away to most people then and their only contact with this strange land would have been through newspaper reports and, in the case of the children, through comics. The whole event would have drawn huge crowds of thousands of spectators and it would have been talked about for many years after.

# The Romans and their connection with the area

Plymouth didn't exist when the Romans created Exeter though there is evidence that they occupied the area.

Roman Way leading downwards from Kings Tamerton is said to be the route that the Romans took on their way to Cornwall. A Roman signalling station is thought to have existed at the top of the hill. Roman Way was previously called, 'Old Wall's Lane' in the 1800s, which would suggest an earlier settlement. The area was excavated in 1934 by a Mr E N Masson Phillips who discovered an early fortification. Soapwort has been found growing nearby and this was a herb used by the Romans and is usually only found on the site of an old settlement.

Roman Way lies on the second oldest route traceable in Plymouth which travels east to west from Saltash to Plympton. There seems to be no record of Roman coins being found at Roman Way although a hoard of Roman coins was found at Compton Giffard in 1894 and this lies on the same route. The hoard contained a thousand coins and none were later than AD 280. It was suggested by the British Museum that the coins could have been used to pay the Romans who were stationed in the area at the time. A similar hoard was found at Marazion near Penzance. Roman coins have also been found at Whitleigh and by the Plym.

Many people believe that Stonehouse got its name from an ancient stone house, now long gone, which once stood in the area. Stonehouse was named by the Saxons who must have been referring to the ruin of a previous civilisation. If that was the case, then only the Romans would have had the ability to build it.

The Romans left Britain in 410AD.

In the early 1980s, the Evening Herald reported the find of a Roman coin on the shores of the River Plym. The article read:

**'Eighteen hundred years ago this coin must have been lost on the shores of the River Plym. It has been identified as a bronze 'as' and depicts on one side Antoninus Pius, who was Emperor of Rome from 138 to 161 AD, and on the other, Annona, the goddess of the corn-harvest.**
**This valuable clue to Plymouth's past was found recently, in the mud of the River Plym near Marsh Mills by Peter Jones, 15, of Efford who was digging not for Romans but for worms.'**

There must be many more artefacts and coins to be found, perhaps buried in back gardens and farmers fields. I've known people who have found such coins but it seems quite a rare occurrence although I'm sure there is much still to be found.

# Mudlarking

In Victorian times, a mudlark was someone who searched along the banks of the Thames for anything that had washed up and could be sold. The practice was usually taken up by children or widows with no income. They would be lucky if they made a penny a day selling what they found. Today, mudlarking is a popular pastime and people still search the shores of the Thames for the 'big find'. A licence costs £7.50 a day and finds can date back hundreds or even thousands of years to Roman times.

You don't have to live in London to go mudlarking though. It's possible to find artefacts dating back to Roman times on the shores of the Plym and many farmland areas used 'Dock Dung' which was a collection of all the rubbish from Plymouth including pottery, bottles, jars, clay pipes as well as more unsavoury produce such as horse droppings, night soil and offal etc. The latter was seen as perfect manure for farmer's fields and it could be bought by the ton. It would then be transported from Plymouth by barge up river to any farm that had access to the water. Special wooden jetties were built where the dung could be sorted. All the sharp items such as bottles, pipes, pottery etc was taken out by workers and thrown into the nearby marsh. The dung was then carried in wicker baskets to

nearby fields. It was quite a profitable exercise and the returning barges would carry back stone or farm produce. The sorted pottery and bottles etc have lain in the mud ever since and it's possible to find clay pipes, Codd bottles, clay ink wells, clay marmalade jars, the remnants of old Victorian shoes and , if you're lucky, even coins.

These jetties are found all over but have all rotted away over time. Part of the jetty still remains on the river bank at Church Town Farm near Saltash and there are thousands of pieces of pottery from the turn of the 20th Century nearby. Other areas where there are finds in abundance are at Antony Passage, Forder, Ernesettle Creek and Tamerton Foliot Creek. Clay pipes from the 1600s have been found at Empacombe and many other finds date back hundreds of years.

I've mudlarked at Churchtown Farm, Antony Passage and  Moditonham Quay and searched for pottery shards on farmer's fields including those at Empicombe. There's something very rewarding about finding something discarded maybe a hundred years ago but if you're rummaging in the mud, it's a smelly and filthy pastime and whatever you find will inevitable be broken. Some Codd Bottles can be found complete though as can stoneware Marmalade jars and ink wells etc. Many people research maps and books to discover where old Victorian dumps lie and will dig them in the dead of night, presumably to avoid getting in any trouble, and produce great finds, many which appear to turn up on ebay and at local car boot sales! In the 1970s, there used to be a mound on the way to Laira School which I was informed was an old Victorian dumping ground. It could clearly be seen and was regularly dug by bottle collectors. Nowadays, it's all be flattened and built over but there are many more all over the region still to be found and many diggers will go out in the dead of night to their newly discovered secret locations, complete with spades, to see what they can turn up.

It's an interesting pastime and there's allsorts to be found. Try not to upset the locals though!

# Laurel and Hardy

When I was a boy, I loved watching Laurel and Hardy on the tv on Saturday mornings. Perhaps not too many people know that Laurel and Hardy once appeared at the Palace Theatre. The date was the 17th of May, 1954 and Stan and Ollie were touring the country appearing in a show called, 'Birds of a Feather'. The shows in Plymouth were to have been their last shows of the tour. Playing on the same bill at the time were Harry Worth and 'Wonder Horse Tony'. Unfortunately, Oliver Hardy had a severe bout of the flu and also had a mild heart attack and the show was cancelled. Ollie spent the rest of his stay in Plymouth recovering at the Grand Hotel on the Hoe.

Laurel and Hardy had visited Britain once before in 1932 when they were mobbed wherever they went. When they returned in 1954 they were handicapped by age and illness but still managed to give an exhausting thirteen shows a week.

After they had to pull out from the show, Stan Laurel wrote a letter to the manager of the Palace Theatre, William Willis, apologising. It read:

**'My Dear Mr Willis,**

**Please pardon delay in acknowledgement of your kind letter of the 22nd.inst. which was deeply appreciated. Many many thanks.**

**Mr Hardy is feeling better but, of course, is still very weak. However, we are sailing for the States on June 2nd, so I think the voyage and rest will do him a lot of good.**

**We too were very much disappointed, not being able to fulfil our engagement with you - unfortunate for all concerned, could have been a profitable and happy week. Anyway, we hope to have the opportunity and pleasure of meeting and playing for you again in the near future.**

**Mrs Laurel and Mr and Mrs Hardy join in kindest regards and every good wish always, and remember us kindly to Mr Heath, the staff and regular patrons.**

**Very Sincerely:**

**Stan Laurel.'**

# Gog and Magog

One of the earliest recorded mentions of the Hoe area comes from Geoffrey of Monmouth who wrote about Plymouth Hoe in 1136 when he told the story of the giant, Gogmagog (which he originally calls Goemagot). The story of Gogmagog's Leap told how Brutus, the great-grandson of the Trojan hero, Aeneas, came to Albion with his followers and decided to settle. He called the land 'Britain' which was meant to be a derivation of 'Brutus'. Brutus drove out the giants who inhabited the land sending them into the mountains in the west. One day, while holding a festival at the port where they first landed, Brutus and his men were attacked by a group of giants who they killed all except one who was called Gogmagog. He was said to be 12 cubits high. A cubit would have been about one and a half feet which would have made Gogmagog about 18 feet tall. It was said that Gogmagog could wield an uprooted oak tree as a weapon. Brutus kept Gogmagog alive so that he could wrestle with Corineus, the then Duke of Cornwall, who loved to wrestle

with giants. When the opponents met for the first time, Gogmagog gripped Corineus so tightly around his middle that he broke three of his ribs. This enraged Corineus who then threw Gogmagog off nearby cliffs and he fell to his death on the jagged rocks below. This was all said to have happened on Plymouth Hoe and the chalk giants that once appeared on the Hoe represented this wrestling match.

There is a record of the chalk cut giant being on Plymouth Hoe in 1486 and a record in the City Archive shows a receipt for a bill for cleaning and weeding the giant. The bill was paid by the Earl of Edgcumbe. It is uncertain when the figure first appeared. Town records from 1486 onwards call the figure Gogmagog but in Carew's Survey of Cornwall in 1602, he refers to there being two figures on the slopes of the Hoe, both wielding clubs. One was bigger than the other and he calls them Gog and Magog, splitting the name into two halves. Several years later though, the smaller figure was being referred to as Corineus so the figures obviously commemorated the earlier wrestling match mentioned by Geoffrey of Monmouth . The figures were unfortunately destroyed when the Citadel was built in the reign of King Charles II.

# Saltash Passage and the US Army Base, 1944

In January 1944, the US Army set up camp at Vicarage Road in preparation for the D-Day landings. Altogether, it housed 60,000 troops on their way to the Normandy landings. It was also a reception centre for returning troops from July 1944.

The whole operation was highly secret and from May 1944, anyone who wanted to visit relatives in the area had to apply for a permit and would be escorted to the address by military police. They would also have to give a specific time when they would be leaving.

The mission was codenamed Operation Overlord. The codename for the many US bases around Plymouth was 'sausages'.

During this time, the river was full of ships loading men and equipment. One day, the river was full of ships and the next day, it was completely empty as the troops headed towards the beaches of Normandy.

Children in the area loved the American troops and would pester them for sweets, chewing gum, chocolate, food and cocoa etc. The Americans weren't affected by rationing and were very generous to the locals especially the children. In the city, they even paid for and organised parties for them.

The large majority of troops in Plymouth were from the 29th Armoured division which went on to land at the Omah and Utah beaches. Omah beach was the codename for one of the main landing points for the troops on 6 June 1944. Unfortunately, it is where the Americans suffered their heaviest casualties. The Vicarage Road camp was decommissioned in September 1945.

Tamar Terrace was later renamed Normandy Way and Vicarage Road was renamed Normandy Hill to commemorate the troops that passed this way on their way to the D-Day landings.

A monument stands in Saltash Passage to commemorate where a slipway was built for the departure of the US troops. They constructed slipways or 'hards' which were known as 'chocolate box hards' to the troops. Sections can still be seen there, some are scattered along the foreshore.

A tablet commemorating the event was unveiled on Normandy Hill, known as US Army Route 23, by the Mayor of Cherbourg in May 1947.

A memorial was later erected in the gardens and the plaque on it reads: 'This tablet marks the departure from this place of units of the V and V11 corps of the United States Army on the 6th June 1944 for the D-Day landings in France and was unveiled by His Excellency John Hay Whitney, the Ambassador of the United States of America. May 1958'.

# Dancing on the Hoe

Al fresco dancing on the Hoe began during the first week of May 1941 and was a success from the beginning. The idea was first suggested by the Lord Mayor, Lord Astor. Lady Nancy Astor regularly took part and among her dancing partners was the Duke of Kent. The dancing raised people's spirits and brought everyone together.

Noel Coward, who was a friend of the Astors, said at the time, 'After all that devastation, on a Summer evening, people were dancing on the Hoe. It made me cry - the bravery, the gallantry, the Englishness of it!' The dances continued for many years. A huge dance was held on the Hoe at the end of the war to celebrate VE Day.

Lady Astor was born in America in 1879.She married Waldorf Astor in 1906 and they lived at 3 Elliot Terrace on the Hoe. She was the MP for Sutton from 1919 to 1945. During the Second World War, Lord and Lady Astor were the Mayor and Lady Mayor of Plymouth.

Lady Astor was well known for her straight to the point way of talking. She once said to Winston Churchill, 'If I was your wife I would give you poison!' to which Churchill replied, 'If I was your husband, I'd drink it!' Lady Astor died in 1964.

Lady Astor dancing with a sailor on Plymouth Hoe.

# The Great Liners

Plymothians would line the docks in the hope of seeing famous passengers disembark from the many ocean liners that called at Millbay. The Queen Mary was Cunard's pride and joy and famous passengers who docked at Plymouth on The Queen Mary included Gloria Swanson and Jack Warner who both arrived in the city in 1938.

The Mauretania came to Plymouth regularly and delivered passengers and mail to the city. Film stars were quite often amongst the passengers and these included the American crooner, Bing Crosby. The Mauretania was built by Swan, Hunter and Wigham in Newcastle in 1907. It was the world's fastest liner from 1907 to 1927 and was part of Cunard Line's Liverpool to New York service.

Charlie Chaplin disembarked from the Mauretania in 1931 to the delight of many Plymothians that had come to see him. The star of many silent films, he made his famous film, 'City Lights' in the same year. Whilst in Plymouth, Chaplin was the guest of Nancy Astor at her home in Elliott Terrace on the Hoe. Also visiting Astor at the same time were Amy Johnson and George Bernard Shaw. The Mauretania made it's final eastwards crossing on September 1934, from New York to Southampton and was sent to the breakers yard in July 1935.

The Normandie steamed into Plymouth Sound in 1937 after crossing the Atlantic in a record breaking time. The Normandie (pictured) was the industry's first 1,000 ft ocean liner. Walt Disney was among the many famous passengers who landed at Plymouth. The liner capsized and caught fire in New York while being converted for use in the Second World War.

Liner passengers would start their onward journey to London from Millbay Station. Many film stars including George Raft and Charlie Chaplin would board the trains there with thousands of less famous travellers. The station and hotels were built to accommodate the many visitors.

The days of the great ocean liners calling at Plymouth are now long gone but occasionally one drops anchor in the Sound but they are few and far between.

# Plymouth Argyle

Argyle played their first full game in 1886. Their captain was F Howard Grose and the team met at Grose's home in Argyll Terrace. Originally called Argyle Athletic, they were named after Grose's admiration for the playing skills of the Argyll and Sutherland Highlanders regimental team. They originally only played away games as they had no pitch of their own and their practice sessions took place at Freedom Fields. In 1901, they started playing at the ground at Home Park which had been built for the Devonport Albion Rugby Club. In the first two years, Home Park was also the home to whippet racing and cycling tournaments. In 1903, they were allowed to join the Southern League and they then played their first game as Plymouth Argyle.

The photo shows the team in 1922. Back row: J Devine, F Cosgrove, J Muir, W Cook, P Corcoran, W Frost, J Little, C Miller. Second row: F Haynes (trainer), I Leathlean, J Hill, J Logan, R Jack (sec. man) J Jobson, C Eastwood, S Atterbury (assistant trainer). Seated: J Dickinson, B Bowler, H Batten, H Kirk, M Russell, W Forbes, H Raymond, W Baker, A Rowe. Front row: J Kirkpatrick, J Fowler, J Walker, T Gallogley, F Richardson, R Jack, J Leslie and A Wilson.

# The Countess of Edgcumbe's pet pig

The Countess of Mount Edgcumbe, Emma Gilbert, had a pet pig which she called Cupid.
Cupid led a charmed life eating at the dinner table of the Edgcumbes and even accompanying the Countess, Emma Gilbert, on trips to London. The Edgcumbes love of their pets can be seen at Fern Dell where many of them are buried. When a later Countess of Mount Edgcumbe, Caroline Georgia, died in 1909, she requested that a fountain be erected near the shore at Cremyll which bore the inscription, 'For the Doggies'.
When Cupid died in 1768, it was said that he was buried in a gold casket beneath the Obelisk at Cremyll.

A Kingsbrige man wrote a poem about Cupid on hearing of it's demise. It read:
'Oh dry those tears so round and big,
Nor waste in sight your precious wind,
Death only takes a little pig
Your Lord and Son are still behind.'
Cupid's resting place is a mystery though, as it appears to have once had a grave at Fern Dell. However, a monumental urn dedicated to the pig has long since disappeared.
On one of his visits to Mount Edgcumbe, George III, on seeing Cupid's headstone, remarked to Queen Charlotte, 'It's the family vault, Charley! The family vault!'

# The Honicknowle Carnival

The Honicknowle Carnival started in 1933. This photo shows the Maypole Dancers on their cart ready to take part in the Carnival of 1934. Pictured in Butt Park Road, this photo includes Constance Brimacombe, Winnie and Lily Lee, Beryl Ivey, Millie Shears, Joyce Chapman and Mary McKee. The annual carnival was organised by Edgar Lewis and attracted thousands of people from all over the city. In the days before the building of the many housing estates in the 1950s, Honicknowle was a very different place with farms, quarries, a brick works and many open spaces. The nearby Woodland Fort housed troops and at different times, also housed families and was used for recreational purposes.

Events in the Carnival included maypole dancing (very popular at the time), ladies football, children's competitions, fancy dress shows and various sports events. A Carnival Queen would preside over events. In 1933, the Queen was Hilda Pearn. In 1934, the Queen was Florence Ivey and in 1935, Agnes Lewis had the honour. The Parade was a very popular part of the Carnival and included horses and carts from local farmers as well as local residents.

In 1939, Honicknowle Week, as the Carnival was known, ceased for nine years because of the Second World War. In that year, Joyce Chapman was Queen. The Carnival was revived in 1948 and attracted more attention than it had in previous years because of the growth of housing in the area. The 1949 carnival included wagons and decorated horses. Thirteen Carnival Queens from other parts of the City took part in the parade and there were 130 entrants in the fancy dress parade. Joan Slater, who was Miss Honicknowle, presented the first prize to Valerie Steele and also presented the prizes for the juvenile talent contest. The day ended with old time dancing and an al fresco dance in the street. The Carnival seemed to end once the new housing estates were built in the 1950s. The village life that was once Honicknowle had now gone. Farms were built on and the brickworks was eventually knocked down. A way of life had suddenly changed forever.

# Scott of the Antarctic

Robert Falcon Scott was born in Plymouth on the 6 June 1868. He was a British Naval Officer and explorer who led two expeditions to Antarctica. The first, the Discovery Expedition, lasted three years and began in 1901. His second expedition, the Terra Nova Expedition, which commenced in 1910, is more well known and was the expedition where, unfortunately, he lost his life. Scott led a team of five men in a race to reach the South Pole. When he arrived on the 17 January 1912, he discovered that he had been beaten to the position by the Norwegian, Roald Amundsen and his team. Scott and his team, which included Edward Wilson, H R Bowers, Lawrence Oates and Edgar Evans, made their way back but died of a combination of the cold, hunger and exhaustion.

Scott was born at Outlands House, the family home, in the Parish of Stoke Damerel. He was a distant descendant of Sir Walter Scott and he was the father of the naturalist, Peter Scott. Outlands has now gone and St Bartholomew's Church stands in its place. Within the church is a piece of wood bearing Scott's name. In 1908, Scott had carved his name on a tree at Outlands from where the wood was taken.

Scott was 43 when he died and his body, and that of his comrades, remain at the camp where he was found. A wooden cross was erected on top of a high cairn of snow which covered the camp.

A memorial stands to Scott at Mount Wise in Devonport.

# Mary Newman

It is interesting that Mary Newman's Cottage is in Culver Road, Saltash because she almost certainly never lived there. Mary married Francis Drake on the 4th July, 1569 at the church at Higher St Budeaux and this is recorded in the parish records. The records also show the marriages of three other women with the name Newman between 1552 and 1571, within the St Budeaux Parish, and it is assumed that they were all related.

Stories passed from generation to generation by word of mouth say that Mary was born at Agaton Farm and was the daughter of the important Newman family. However, John Drake, the cousin of Francis, in a

deposition to Spanish inquisitors in 1587, stated that Mary was born in London. It has been suggested that Mary was actually the sister of Drake's shipmate, Harry Newman, who it is recorded, came from St Budeaux.

Little seems to have been written down about Mary and much of her life is a mystery. There are said to be no pictures of Mary but, with her being married to such an important figure of the day, a painting may well exist, perhaps mistakenly listed as someone else. It has also been suggested that Mary, who would have been brought up in the parish of St Budeaux, may have lived at the old barn that still stands off Normandy Hill (see picture). Although the barn is from the 1500s, there seems to be little to support the story although it would be a better bet than the house in Saltash.

Drake was knighted in 1581 and was elected Mayor of Plymouth in the same year. Mary became Lady Drake and Mayoress. Drake bought Buckland Abbey in 1581 and they both lived there for a while. They had previously lived at Looe Street in Plymouth. Mary, however, died two years later in 1583.

Two funeral services were held for Mary. One was at St Andrew's Church and the other was at St Budeaux, where her body was said to have been buried. Today, there is no sign of her grave at St Budeaux and past attempts to find it have failed.

Sir Francis Drake and Mary Newman had no children and there are no direct descendants of Drake. He married Elizabeth Sydenham in 1585. Sir Francis Drake died in 1596 of dysentery while anchored off Panama. He was just 56 years old. He was buried at sea in a lead coffin off the Portobello coast.

# The Silver Mine under Saltash Passage

Many people walking around Saltash Passage today might notice the subsidence that appears in the area. The wall beside The Ferry House Inn has been cordoned off for some time now. Above the wall, the path, serving the houses above, is falling away. This subsidence was thought to have been explained many years ago when local historian, Marshall Ware, suggested that this was the area where the pipe from the American fuel tank, kept in the old orchard, ran down towards the quay. However, subsidence has also been noticed in Little Ash Gardens and near the old wall facing the River Tamar. Even further up the road at Vicarage Gardens the pavement is showing signs of sinking.

A house in Little Ash Gardens has had to be under-pinned in the past and this all seems to be due to the underground mining that once took place in the area.

In 1837, Charles Trelawny excavated for lead-silver deposits under Saltash Passage. The mine tunnel ran from Kinterbury Creek under, what is now, the main road and up towards the quarry that is now Little Ash Gardens. It is believed that the house affected lies above this mine as does many of the homes within the area. With the disturbance of the bombing during the Second World War (a armaments barge was hit on the River Tamar), the mineshaft was probably disturbed.

Many years ago, the entrance to the mineshaft was sealed up to stop children from entering. The mines are still there but remain a secret to many visitors to the area.

# Titanic Survivors

WHITE STARLINER TITANIC.
LEAVING SOUTHAMPTON DOCKS,
APRIL 10th 1912.

On 28 April 1912, the Titanic survivors were brought back to Millbay Docks, fourteen days after the ship had sank. At 8am, the SS Lapland moored at Cawsand Bay with the 167 members of the Titanic who hadn't been detained in New York for the American inquiry. Three tenders left Millbay Docks to collect the passengers and the 1,927 sacks of mail that had been scheduled to be carried by the Titanic. The third tender, the Sir Richard Grenville, carrying the survivors, killed time in the Sound while the dock labourers and porters were paid off and escorted out of the dock gates at West Hoe. After midday, the tender was given the all clear and the survivors were allowed to disembark in an air of secrecy. They were then put on a special train from Millbay Docks to Southampton where they arrived at 10.10pm that night.

# Little Ash Tea Gardens in Saltash Passage

Little Ash Tea Gardens was once a very popular beauty spot and was visited by over twenty thousand people in one year. Now long gone, its location would have been at the far end of where Little Ash Gardens now stands.

In the background of this photo, steps lead down from near to the fields at the Kloof. With the steep bank, it's easy to imagine this as Little Ash Quarry. Although it's hard to see, there are huge queues of people both on the steps and at the top of the steep drop.

In the picture, there is a larger tent, with Little Ash Tea Gardens painted on the top in large letters, and a smaller tent with seats laid out underneath. Several large flag poles, with flags flying, mark its location. All around, there are coloured bunting flags and also a wooden picket fence along the edge. The van on the left of the picture belongs to a company called, 'Day'.

A programme of music was played by the band of the Plymouth Corporation Tramways and Transport. The conductor of the band, in the 1920s, was a Mr C E Lewenden and some of the tunes of the day that were played included; 'She Don't Wanna', 'I Want to be Alone with Mary Brown' and 'Trail of the Tamarind Tree'. Some of the patrons who attended the event included Vice-Admiral Sir Rudolph Bentinck, Major Leslie Hore-Belisha MP and Rear Admiral Oliver Backhouse, as well as

**Little Ash Gardens,**
SALTASH PASSAGE,
("Devonport's Beauty Spot") re-open for the season
early in APRIL.

*Beautiful Grounds,* *Large Meadow,*
*Swings, Roundabout, See-Saws, Etc.*

*The ideal place for* Sunday School Outings

AMPLE ACCOMMODATION FOR SMALL OR LARGE
PARTIES.
HIGH-CLASS TEAS AND REFRESHMENTS
AT POPULAR PRICES

*Frequent Cars from Stuart Road, Morice Square and*
*Tor Lane. Return Fare,* 5d. ; *Children,* 3d.

*For Tea Tariff, Special Cars, & all Particulars:*
Apply to THE MANAGER,
Devonport & District Tramways Co.,
Milehouse, Devonport.

*N.B.—These GARDENS were visited last Summer by*
*nearly* **20,000** *persons.*

many other Naval Officers. Combined with the Regatta, it was quite an event.

Here's an advert for the Tea Gardens. It was then described as Devonport's beauty spot (Saltash Passage, at the time, was classed as part of Devonport). It served high class teas and refreshments, had brass bands and park rides such as swings, roundabouts and see-saws. Frequent tramcars ran from Stuart Road, Morice Square and Tor Lane. The return fare for adults was 5d and for children 3d. Advertised as the ideal place for Sunday School outings.

The Officials included the Lord Mayor who, in the 1920s, was Councillor W H Priest, G A Daymond of Mount Tamar Villas and Walter Wyatt of Baden Terrace. James Ware who lived at the Kloof, was treasurer until ill health stopped him taking part after 1928.

# The Beatles

The Beatles appeared at the ABC on the 13th November, 1963. While in Plymouth, the Beatles were interviewed for a tv show made by Westward Television called, 'Move Over, Dad!' The interviewer was Stuart Hutchison. So many fans blocked the street that the Beatles had to be taken through a tunnel, from the ABC to Westward Studios, to be interviewed. The concert very nearly didn't take place as Paul had been suffering from gastric flu and their booked appearance at Portsmouth on the previous night was cancelled because of this.

Below is a transcript of the Beatles interview with Stuart Hutchison;
Hutchison: 'Well Paul, how are you after your collapse we read about?'
Paul: 'I didn't really collapse. That was just the naughty newspapers,
writing it. Misquote! Nah, I just had a bit of flu, you know. I'm fine today,
thank you.'
Hutchison: 'You're feeling alright?'
Paul: (in a comical voice) 'Lovely. Real lovely.'
Hutchison: 'How are the rest of you? How are you going to avoid
catching...?'
John: (in a pathetic voice) 'We're fine, thank you.'
George: 'Oh, we're OK. Yeah, great.'
Hutchison: 'Are you taking any cold prevention, now?'
Paul: 'Yeah, I'm taking 'em all. Got 'em all.'
John: (quietly) 'It's only 1/6 a tube.'
(Paul giggles)
Hutchison: 'How about these escape plans you keep beating about? You
got out of one place disguised as policemen.'
Beatles: 'No, no!'
George: 'We didn't, actually. We put the policemen's helmets on...'
Paul: 'Just for a laugh, you know.'
George: 'Yeah.'

Paul: 'The policemen said, 'Aww, let's have a laugh, and put these helmets...'
George: 'We jumped out of the van, and you know... The press were there to take the photographs, so we jumped out with the helmets on. So the next day it was...'
Paul: 'The next day you read in the papers...'
George: '...here they are, disguised.'
Ringo: 'Have you ever seen a policeman in a corduroy coat?'
John: 'I have. I saw one back in 1832, I think.'
Ringo: 'He knows, you see.'
Hutchison: 'Did you put the helmets on over the haircuts?'
Paul: 'Yeah.'
Ringo: 'Sure.'
John: 'Well, we couldn't put them underneath.'
(Beatles laugh)
Paul: 'And I also read in the papers today, there's a man who said we wear wigs!'
Ringo: (loudly) 'We don't!'
Paul: 'We don't. Honest. Feel it.'
Hutchison: 'True. It's lovely, yes. Oh, on this program a few weeks ago, somebody said the Beatles haircut was going out because the fringe was so long you couldn't see the birds. What comment have you got to make on that?'
John: (yells) 'It's a dirty lie!'
George: (laughs)
Paul: 'We can see quite well. I can see quite well, thanks, John.'
George: 'Well, some of us can.'
(laughter)
Hutchison: 'Are you looking forward to doing it tonight?'
Beatles: 'Yeah!
Paul: 'Of course.'
Hutchison: 'Well, they've all been looking forward to seeing you, and they're out there now. Thank you very much, boys.'
Beatles: 'Thank you.'
John: 'Pleasure.'
The Beatles visited the ABC again on the 29th October, 1964.
The Beatles visited a third time in September 1967 while filming the Magical Mystery Tour and pictures appear of them sitting on the Hoe overlooking the Sound.

# Charles Darwin

At Devil's Point, at the end of Durnford Street, there is a plaque commemorating the sailing from Barn Pool, at Mount Edgcumbe, of HMS Beagle.

Charles Darwin's journey is mentioned in the Quarterly Review of 1840: 'On the 27th November, 1831, the well-manned, well-appointed and well-provided Beagle sailed from Barn Pool, and having circumnavigated the globe, and accomplished all the objects the expedition had in view, as far was practical, she anchored at Falmouth on the 2nd October, 1836, after an absence of four years and nine months.'

Darwin had lived in Plymouth for two months before his famous voyage around the world in HMS Beagle. The ship was captained by Robert Fitzroy. Darwin, who was then just 22 years old, joined the crew as a naturalist. He had a wealthy family who paid the £30 fare needed to travel on the Beagle.

When he returned to England, he married Emma Wedgwood, the daughter of the potter, Josiah Wedgwood.
He carried on his research and in 1859, his book, 'The Origin of the Species by Natural Selection' was published.
Darwin died in 1882 at his home in Orpington, Kent. He is buried at Westminster Abbey.

# Kiss me, Hardy

Vice-Admiral Sir Thomas Masterman Hardy once lived at 156 Durnford Street. Although he rose through the ranks to become a Vice-Admiral, his Naval career is remembered by just three words, 'Kiss me Hardy'. When Vice-Admiral Horatio Nelson was fatally wounded aboard HMS Victory in 1805, he was taken below deck where he was later visited by Hardy.

Nelson's words to him were, 'Take care of poor Lady Hamilton', before he uttered the immortal words, 'Kiss me, Hardy'. It has been suggested that what Nelson actually said was, 'Kismet, Hardy' meaning that this was his fate. However, that was not the case as many officers present, including his surgeon, William Beatty, who wrote down his words, bore witness to the actual event. When Nelson uttered the words, 'Kiss me, Hardy', Hardy knelt beside him and kissed him on the cheek. Many people think that these were his last words, but, his final words were uttered just before he died three hours after he had been shot. These words were, 'God and my country'.

A young sailor from Cawsand, Lieutenant John Pollard, was a midshipman on the Victory when Nelson was fatally wounded. Although not a well known name now, it was Pollard who shot and killed the enemy sailor who shot Nelson. He was known thereafter as, 'Nelson's Avenger'. However, several other men also claimed to have shot the Frenchman.

In An Authentic Narrative of the Death of Lord Nelson by Sir William Beatty, published in 1807, he wrote:

'There were only two Frenchmen left alive in the mizzen-top of the Redoubtale at the time of his Lordship's being wounded and by the hands of these he fell. At length one of them was killed by a musket ball; and the other, then attempting to make his escape from the top down the rigging, Mr Pollard (Midshipman) fired his musket at him and shot him in the back when he fell dead from the shrouds on the Redoutable's poop.'

Beatty's account supports Pollard being the 'avenger'.

# The Blitz of 1941

During the Second World War, the heaviest attacks on the city came in 1941. In the two intensive attacks on the 20 and 21 March, 336 people lost their lives. Five further attacks in April brought the toll to 590.

There was hardly a building in Plymouth that wasn't touched in some way by the Blitz. Much of the city centre was obliterated and although many buildings remained amongst the debris, most were damaged beyond repair.

It's hard now to imagine the total devastation the bombing caused. Many of the most popular streets, Bedford Street, Union Street, Old Town Street, Frankfort Street, Cornwall Street, George Street etc were either totally destroyed or severely damaged. Major buildings such as the Guildhall, the Municipal Buildings, St Andrew's Church, Charles Church and the General Post Office were obliterated.

Many schools were also hit. These included Plymouth High School for Girls, the Hoe Grammar School and the infants school at Summerland Place. Many churches were destroyed also including St James the Less, King Street Methodist, St Peter's, George Street Baptist and many others. The bombing was indiscriminate and destroyed anything that got in its way.

In the dockyard, the bombing was bad but not as damaging as would have been thought and within a few months, it was back to 90% efficiency.

Outside the city, the bombing was just as devastating and areas affected included Devonport, Stonehouse, St Budeaux, Swilly and Saltash Passage. Devonport lost many buildings including the Post Office, the Alhambra Theatre, the Synagogue, the Hippodrome and the Salvation Army Headquarters.

Residential houses that were either destroyed or beyond repair amounted to 3,754.Others that were seriously damaged but able to be repaired amounted to 18,398. Houses that were slightly damaged amounted to an additional 49,950.

It's hard to imagine today, unless you've lived through it, such devastation to a city.

Many children were packed off to live with relatives, friends or obliging families in safe areas in the countryside. Thousands left on special trains and many saw it as an adventure while others were upset to leave their parents behind. Lady Astor said at the time, 'What helped the evacuation was that everyone seemed to have a cousin in the country!'.

News of the devastation of Plymouth soon reached the rest of the world and gifts arrived from all over particularly the United States who sent ambulances, soft toys, food packages and surgical dressings. The Royal Sailors Rest received crates of supplies so large that they were unable to get them into the building.

At the end of the war, there were a total of 4,448 casualties due to the raids and heavy bombing of the city.

Throughout it all though, the people of Plymouth remained strong and there were regular dances on the Hoe almost in defiance of the enemy as they bombed the city.

Plymouth was reborn after the war and the city was rebuilt almost from scratch. Few buildings remained in the heart of the city that were there before the war and even now, the city is constantly changing.

# Lawrence of Arabia

T E Lawrence was stationed at Mount Batten in Plymouth and was posted to RAF Cattewater during March 1929 and stayed in Plymouth until 1935 where he worked on high-speed boats.

Previously, at the beginning of the First World War, Lawrence had been a university post-graduate researcher and had travelled extensively within the Ottoman Empire. When he volunteered his services, he was posted to Cairo. Lawrence fought with the Arab troops against the enemy forces of the Ottoman Empire. In 1918, he was involved in the capture of Damascus and was promoted to Lieutenant Colonel. After the War, his fame spread and he became known as Lawrence of Arabia.

When he joined the RAF in 1922, he enlisted as John Hume Ross to protect his identity. This was discovered in 1923 and he was forced out of the RAF. He changed his name to T E Shaw and enlisted in the Royal Tank Corps. He was unhappy there and petitioned the RAF to re-accept him, which they did in 1925.

He died aged 46 in a motor bike accident near his cottage in Wareham. There is a plaque at Turnchapel which commemorates Lawrence. It reads:

'Lawrence of Arabia 1888-1935.

On his return from India in 1929 T E Lawrence, under the assumed name of Shaw, was posted to a flying boat squadron at RAF Mount Batten he remained in the marine craft section until his discharge 19 February 1935.'

# The Ferry House Inn

The original house where the Ferry House Inn stands in Saltash Passage was built in 1575. It was recorded that it was converted into an Inn in 1850. However, in other records, the landlord in 1812 is said to be a Mr John Sole. Perhaps the 1850 date is wrong and maybe it should be 1805. The Inn got its name from the ferry that left from the slipway opposite. Before the building of the Royal Albert Bridge, the ferry ran along the route of the bridge and not from the front of the Ferry House Inn which may suggest that the Inn had a different name originally. The history of the Inn itself seems very scant although there is much recorded about the ferry.

The ferry ran for at least six hundred years and carried passengers across the Tamar long before the Inn or the building existed.

Daniel Defoe, the author of Robinson Crusoe, crossed here in 1724 and wrote, 'the Tamar here is very wide, and the ferry boats bad, so that I thought myself well escaped when I got safe on shore in Cornwall.'

For many years, the Inn has provided food and drink for passengers on their way to Cornwall via the ferry.

It is still open for business although the last ferry ran in October 1961 the day before the Tamar Bridge opened to traffic.

The Inn is said to be haunted but no-one knows by who. Perhaps it's the ghost of an earlier landlord, the aptly named John Sole.

# Plymouth Trams

Transport played a big part in linking the three towns. Plymouth's first tramway was opened in 1872 by the Plymouth, Stonehouse and Devonport Tramways Company. Before the advent of electricity, the trams were pulled by horses. The 4ft 8 inch track ran from Derry's Clock, along Union Street, over Stonehouse Bridge and ended at Cumberland Gardens in Devonport. In 1874, the line was extended to run to Fore Street in Devonport. Electric trams took over from the horse drawn ones in the early 1900's and the service eventually covered most of the area known today as Plymouth.

The photo shows a tram at Saltash Passage in about 1923. Saltash Passage would have been the last stop by the river before this tram headed off back into the town. In 1923, the line was extended from St Budeaux along a track that had been closed since the First World War. The trip from the Pier to Saltash Passage covered a remarkable 9 miles and was the longest journey in the city. The fare was 4d. This one's

marked 'Theatre' and its final destination would have been by Derry's Clock. By 1922, motor buses were running in the city and trams became a less viable proposition. In 1941, only the tramline from Drake's Circus to Peverell was still in use but this was discontinued after the war and the city's last tram ran on 29th September 1945.

# Sir Arthur Conan Doyle

Sir Arthur Conan Doyle assisted at a medical practice at Durnford Street and Sherlock Holmes was said to be based on his colleague, Dr Budd. Conan Doyle achieved the titles of Bachelor of Medicine and Master of

Surgery in 1881 and had studied with George Turnavine Budd in Edinburgh. When Budd opened a practice in Durnford Street in 1882, he asked Conan Doyle to join him. The partnership didn't last long. Although Budd and Conan Doyle were friends, Conan Doyle found his partner over prescribed drugs for his patients, for which he charged them, and was unorthodox in the extreme. He wrote and told his mother, Mary, about Budd's ways. She had never been an admirer of his. After two months, the partnership was dissolved because Budd said that it was short of both finances and patients. Conan Doyle discovered later that Budd had found one of his letters to his mother and the real reason for the break up of the partnership was that he had been upset by what he had read.

Conan Doyle left and set up a practice in Southsea with just £10 to his name. At first, it wasn't very successful and, while he was waiting for patients, he wrote his first story featuring Sherlock Holmes, 'A Study in Scarlet.'

Conan Doyle died on the 7th July 1930, aged 71. Today, passages from his works featuring Sherlock Holmes can be found on brass plaques set into the pavement at Durnford Street.

# Westward Television

Westward Television was launched on the 29th April, 1961. The chairman of the company was Peter Cadbury who had previously been on the board of Tyne Tees Television. He named the company after a course in Westward Ho! where he played golf.

The station was based at Derry's Cross within purpose-built studios. Well-known and much loved presenters included Kenneth MacLeod (pictured), Stuart Hutchison, John Doyle, Lawrie Quayle, Roger Shaw, Graham Danton as well as many others.

Westward's flagship programme was Westward Diary which went out at 6pm on Monday to Friday. The three original presenters were Reginald Bosanquet, Barry Westwood and Kenneth MacLeod. Many people may have forgotten that Reginald Bosanquet worked for Westward before becoming an ITN newsreader. Kenneth MacLeod later became the sole anchor man for the show which featured local news in the first half followed by items such as 'Pick of the Post' and 'Picture Puzzle' where people at home had to guess a mystery location to win a prize. In a time when there weren't so many cars, the picture puzzle was harder than it would appear today because many people hadn't been to the places shown. Other popular Westward shows included 'Treasure Hunt' with

Keith Fordyce and 'A Date with Danton' with Graham Danton.
Shows, being live, regularly broke down and I can recall one show where
nothing would work. Lawrie Quayle had just come back from a holiday in
Spain and, as they had no news or anything else to show the public,
Kenneth MacLeod chatted to him for half an hour about his holiday!
Another favourite on Westward Television was Gus Honeybun who
became a favourite with children. There are still Gus Honeybun trains on
Plymouth Hoe though none of today's children will have any knowledge
of him!
When Westward was taken over by TSW in 1982, I think the people of
the Westcountry expected something better but instead they lost
something that had been very special to many people. The channel and
its presenters are still fondly remembered.
Unfortunately, many of the presenters including Ken MacLeod, John
Doyle and Stuart Hutchinson are no longer around although Gus
Honeybun is apparently living happily on Dartmoor somewhere!

# The Bounty

The story of the Mutiny on the Bounty is well known and documented.
There is a link with Fletcher Christian and Plymouth but how accurate it
is, no-one will ever know.
William Bligh (pictured) will always be remembered for the mutiny which
took place on the Bounty in 1789. William Bligh owned a boathouse near

to the Saltash Ferry and probably, at one time, lived there.
Bligh was born at Tinten Manor at St Tudy on 9th September, 1754.
Amazingly, his first sea voyage was on HMS Monmouth when he was
just aged 7, as a servant to the Captain. By 1787, he had sailed with
Captain Cook and had become Captain of the Bounty.

The Bounty's mission was to collect breadfruit plants from Tahiti and
transport them to the West Indies where they were to be grown to provide
a cheap food source for slaves.
Once Fletcher Christian and the crew of the Bounty had experienced the
paradise of Tahiti for five months, collecting and preparing breadfruit
plants, they were understandably not happy about the prospect of their
return to England when the time came to leave.
Tension overflowed once on board and Fletcher Christian took control of
the ship.
Bligh's diary entry for 28th April, 1789, the day of the mutiny, reads:
'Just before sunrise, Mr Christian and the Master at Arms came into my
cabin while I was fast asleep, and seizing me, tied my hands with a cord
and threatened instant death if I made the least noise. I however called
sufficiently loud to alarm the Officers who found themselves equally
secured by sentinels at their doors. Mr Christian had a cutlass and the
others were armed with muskets and bayonets. I was now carried on
deck in my shirt in torture with a severe bandage round my wrists behind
my back, where I found no man to rescue me.'
Fletcher Christian took control of the Bounty and Bligh, and those faithful
to him, were set adrift in a small boat. Bligh, being an excellent navigator

and seaman, guided the 23 ft boat to Tofua and then on to Timor, which was in the hands of the Dutch. He travelled a total of 3,618 nautical miles with just a sextant, a pocket watch but with no maps. He made it back to England in March 1790 where he faced a court martial but was honourably acquitted.

Christian and his crew settled on the island of Pitcairn. Some were later captured but acquitted at trial, some were hanged and some died at sea. Others died of natural causes.

There were various stories telling how Fletcher Christian met his death on Pitcairn. Some said that he had been murdered while others said that he had died of natural causes, committed suicide or gone insane. Rumours went around that he had faked his own death and returned to England. Midshipman Peter Heywood, who had sailed on The Bounty, reportedly saw Fletcher Chrisitan in Plymouth after the mutiny.

# Bowls on the Hoe

Francis Drake was born at Crowndale near Tavistock in around 1540. Perhaps the most famous story connecting Drake with Plymouth Hoe is the one of how he played bowls on 19th July 1588 with his fellow captains. When news was brought to them that the Armada had been spotted off the Lizard, Drake announced that they still had time to finish the game and beat the Spaniards as well. Many people have dismissed the story as a myth and if the game did take place, it wasn't where the current bowling green is on the Hoe today. Interestingly, the game was banned by law at the time and the reason given was that it caused people to neglect their archery practice. It's possible that the rich had private games in their own gardens. Drake had a house with a garden in Looe Street and John Hawkins had a residence closer to the harbour. If the game did take place on the Hoe, it's likely to have been in the area of the much quarried Lambhay Hill where the Citadel now stands which would have also been near to the chalk giants, Gog and Magog. From here, Drake would have had an excellent vantage point of the Sound right across to Rame. In the only remaining copy of Phoenix Britannicus, published in 1624, only 36 years after the event, the story is told as fact and states that the match did indeed take place on the Hoe.

# Benny Baron

There has been a lot of interest in Laurel and Hardy and their appearance at the Palace Theatre on 17th May, 1954. Plymouth's Barry Ewart has a connection with both the comedians, as his grandfather, Benny Baron, taught Stan many of his routines. Although Barry never knew his grandfather, his mother used to tell him stories of when Benny toured the music halls with his partner, Jack Graham.

Barry's uncle, Billy Baron, remembers, 'Stan adopted exactly the facial expressions my father used in his act. He was the one who got everything wrong and used to 'cry' when his partner knocked off his straw boater.'

Barry says, 'In the film the 'Flying Deuces', Babe (Ollie) sings 'Shine On, Harvest Moon' and Stan does a soft shoe shuffle dance routine to the song which was taught to Stan, step for step, by my grandfather and it brings a tear to my eye every time I watch it.'

Barry continues, 'My grandfather first worked with a young Stanley Jefferson (later Stan Laurel) in the early 1900's ( before America beckoned). The first documented production I can find is a juvenile pantomime company run by H B Levy and J E Cardwell. The production was 'The Sleeping Beauty'. My grandfather Benny was older than Stan. Master Stanley Jefferson played Ebeneezer (Golliwog2) and my grandfather played Major Flashlight. Amongst others in the cast were Jack Graham (later to become my grandfather's stage partner in the double act, 'Graham and Baron'). Jack played Colonel Dreadnought. I have in my possession a letter from Stan to my grandfather (at a time when Stan was famous as one half of Laurel and Hardy) and a picture of Stan, Ollie and Benny when they toured during the 1950s. My late mother always used to refer to Stan as Uncle Stan and she told me many stories. My elder brother used to do part of the soft shoe shuffle (my grandfather died before I was born). Apparently, Stan wanted Benny to go to America where, he explained to Benny, it was money for old rope (he was still not famous then) but my grandmother was having none of it saying it was bad enough touring round Northern England and Scotland (mostly) with their by now growing family including my mum (Irene Baron). After a long stint in variety as a double act with Jack Graham my grandfather finally retired from the stage to run a pub in Sunderland called The Boars Head Hotel. Stan always kept in touch with my grandfather.'

Barry adds, 'My grandfather lived in Sunderland and my mother (Irene Baron) came from Sunderland to Plymouth in the early fifties to marry a matelot (my dad). I might add that my mother, when she was young, sang on stage with none other than Judy Garland, albeit in the chorus line, and most of my uncles played in the orchestra pit of the Sunderland Empire , and toured most of the theatres in Northern England.'

# The Palace Theatre

The theatre in Union Street was originally called the New Palace Theatre of Varieties and was opened on the 5th September, 1898. The opening show featured Adele and May Lilian who were billed as the Levey Sisters. They performed Persian and hunting songs and were followed by an acrobatic act called The Six Craggs. Other acts that night included Walter and Edie Cassons who performed a vaudeville act, a comedian called Harry Comlin and a roller skater called Fred Darby. Tickets ranged from one shilling to 2/6 which included three hours of entertainment.
Fire destroyed both the auditorium and stage on the 23rd December, 1898 and the theatre wasn't opened again until May 1899.
There were twice nightly vaudeville shows by 1902 and artists who appeared during the early 1900s included Neil Kenyon billed as a 'scotch' comedian, Robert Williams a sword swinger and Miss Gertie Gitana who sang songs including 'Nellie Dean.'
In 1909, Harry Houdini played at the theatre for a week during August

and drew a huge crowd.

In 1931, Charlie Chaplin, who was in Plymouth as a guest of Nancy Astor, appeared on stage on the 16th November, 1931.

The theatre stayed open during the blitz of 1941 to keep people's spirits up. Acts that appeared that year included Billy Cotton and his band, Tommy Handley, Arthur Lucan (Old Mother Riley), Henry Hall and his Orchestra as well as many less well-known acts. At Christmas of that year, the main show was Robinson Crusoe which starred George Hirstie. The theatre closed in 1949 for redecorating and reopened with the Billy Cotton Bandshow. The theatre closed again in 1954 due to the lack of touring shows. It was offered to the Plymouth City Council in 1956 but they refused to buy it and it closed for five months before reopening in October 1956. It closed suddenly on the 7th February, 1959 during the pantomime, 'Little Miss Muffet' because of lack of interest.

New management took over the theatre in 1961 and it became Palace Theatre (Bingo) Ltd.

The theatre reopened in 1962 with the pantomime, 'Sinbad the Sailor.' In 1965, Arthur Fox, a businessman from Manchester, paid £50,000 for the theatre with the intention of hosting Star Bingo, wrestling (which was very popular at the time) and striptease.

In 1975, it was bought by EMI and opened on the 19th April, 1977 with a performance of 'The Magic Flute.' The theatre struggled and closed on the 27th May, 1980 when it ceased trading and its contents were put up for sale. It reopened on the 16th May 1981 for a review with Danny La Rue but finally closed in 1983 when it became the Academy Disco.

Its fortunes didn't improve and today it remains closed and its shabby appearance hides its varied history. It's amazing to think of the great acts that have appeared there in the past and how many people in Plymouth have been entertained by them.

The theatre is said to be haunted, a rumour started in the early 1960s.

# Robin Hood

Robin Hood wasn't from Plymouth but the actor who played him in the tv series in the 1950s was. Richard Greene was born in Stonehouse on the 25th August, 1918. He appeared in 'The Adventures of Robin Hood' for 143 episodes between 1955 and 1960.

His aunt was Evie Greene, an actress in musical theatre and his parents were both actors with the Repertory Theatre in Plymouth. He was educated in Kensington and left school when he was 18. His stage career began when he played a spear carrier in a version of Julius

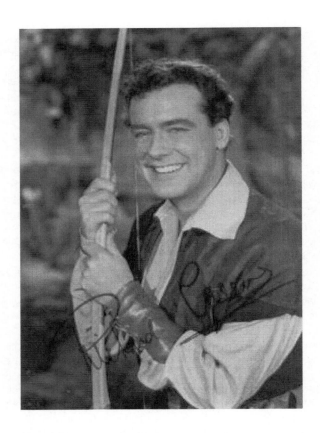

Caesar in 1933. In 1936, he joined the Jevan Brandon Repertory Company and appeared in Terence Rattigan's 'French Without Tears' where he came to the attention of Alexander Korda and Darryl F Zanuck. When he was 20, he joined 20th Century Fox and became a huge success after appearing in John Ford's movie, 'Four Men and a Prayer.' He received so much fan mail that he rivalled Tyrone Power and Robert Taylor. Greene continued to make movies until he enlisted in the 27th Lancers during the Second World War.

Greene appeared in propaganda films during the war and also toured entertaining the troops. However, the war ruined Greene's rising film career although he is well remembered for 'Forever Amber' which was made in 1947. Afterwards, he found himself cast in mainly swashbuckling roles. With little film work and his divorce from Patricia Medina, Greene was almost forgotten when he was approached by Yeoman Films who offered him the lead role in 'The Adventures of Robin Hood.' By taking the role it solved his financial problems and also made him a huge star. Richard Greene died at his home in Norfolk on the 1st June, 1985.

# Red Indians in
# Union Street

When Buffalo Bill visited Plymouth on the 3rd June 1904, he brought with him a troop of Red Indians who toured with his Wild West Show. For the first time, Red Indians could be seen sitting on street corners in the Stonehouse and Union Street areas of the city. It must have been an amazing sight when people's only experience of Red Indians was through stories read about cowboys and Indians in newspapers, comics or seen in early silent movies. Children would have been particularly fascinated by them as their only knowledge of Indians would be from stories heard about Geronimo or Custer's Last Stand.

The one thing that was noted at the time about the visiting Red Indians was that they couldn't handle their drink and notices appeared in drinking houses which read, 'No Indians to be served'. Nowadays, this might seem to appear racist but at the time, the problem was actually caused by them getting drunk too quick and being overly rowdy.

Willie Sitting Bull was one of the Indians who accompanied Buffalo Bill to Britain. He was the only son of Sitting Bull (pictured). Sitting Bull himself had originally taken part in the show when it toured America. It's amazing to think how things had changed in America, especially for the Indians, in just two generations of one family. Willie regularly took part in mock battles which featured the defeat of Custer at Little Big Horn.

The show at the Exhibition Fields, Pennycomequick must have been an amazing sight. It's interesting that there are still people living in Plymouth today that remember their relatives telling them of the Wild West show and a time when Red Indians filled the streets of the town.

# The Mount Edgcumbe Training Ship

The Mount Edgcumbe Industrial Training ship was for homeless and destitute boys. The ship was re-commissioned as a training ship in 1877. It was moored off Saltash Passage but when cables were laid to the North of the Royal Albert Bridge in 1913, it was moved to the Saltash side.

Goshawk, a sea going training vessel, was moored nearby. At the time,

Herbert Price Knevitt was the Superintendent Captain. He was retired from the Navy and lived on board with his wife, Isabella, and their three daughters, Nellie, Nora and Ella. He was 47 at the time and his wife was 35.They also had a servant, Louise Chapman, who was 26, who cooked and kept their quarters tidy. There were also three instructors, the oldest being 62 and the youngest being 34, and a school master, James Sale Gitsham, who was 27. Everyone else on board was referred to as 'inmates' and were all aged between 12 and 16. Some came from Plymouth but they also came from other parts of the country from London to the Isle of Wight.

It wasn't difficult for the boys to find themselves on a training ship. A law in 1884 said that the qualifications for being on the boat were:

Anyone found begging or receiving alms, anyone found wandering who doesn't have a proper home, proper guardianship of means to support themselves; anyone found destitute or who is an orphan or who has a surviving parent who is in prison: anyone who frequents the company of thieves or any child that a parent feels is uncontrollable. However, no boys who had been in prison were allowed on the ship. The payment required for residence was eight shillings per week.

In 1910, Captain H Wesley Harkcom took over the ship and changed the way it had been run for many years. He stopped using the birch on the boys, he moved his family on board and he bought many of the provisions needed from local dealers including food from the Saltash Co-op and coal from Ware's of Saltash Passage. Harkcom was an expert in rowing and encouraged the boys to take up this pastime. The ship also had a brass band and they gave concerts on the green at St Budeaux and in the nearby parish church.

There was said to be anything up to 250 boys on the ship at one time and many went on to see service in the Navy.

On 4 December 1920, the training ship was closed down and was sold on the 18th April, 1921 before being broken up at the Queen Anne Battery.

# The Folly at Mount Edgcumbe

The Folly was built in 1747 and replaced an Obelisk which had stood on the site previously. It was built by using medieval stone from the churches of St George and St Lawrence which once stood in Stonehouse. The same stone was used to build the Picklecombe Seat further along the coast. Part of the seat features a Medieval doorway.

The church of St Lawrence was removed to make way for the Royal William Victualling Yard. The Folly was known as 'The Ruins' for many years. Parts of the old Stonehouse Barrier Gates were also said to have been used. As Stonehouse was never a walled town, it is thought that these came from the Abbey or Manor House.

The Pall Mall Magazine, published in 1897, said:

'The ruin was constructed from the remains of a fallen obelisk and some old granite-work.'

This would suggest that the obelisk had collapsed sometime before the building of the folly in 1747. If parts were used within the construction of the folly then the obelisk erected on Obelisk Hill at Cremyll can't be the complete obelisk that stood where the folly now stands.

An artist painting the scene at the end of the 1800's wrote that the Earl of Edgcumbe had his workers build one folly, had it blown up, didn't like the result and had it built and blown up again to get the result we see today.

The Folly couldn't have pleased everyone and within the pages of A Guide to the Coast of Devon and Cornwall, published in 1859, it says:

'The grounds still are very attractive, but disfigured by silly artificial ruins.'

Also, in Black's Guide to Devonshire, published in 1864, it states:

'Of the mimic ruins scattered through the grounds it is best to take no heed. They are but sorry accessories to a scene which nature has so bounteously enriched.'

Benny Hill appeared at the Palace Theatre on Monday 17th March 1955. Benny was billed as the 'BBC's latest star comedian.' He was born Alfred Hawthorne Hill, in Southampton, on the 21st January 1924. Before becoming a comedian, his jobs had included being a milkman, a bridge operator, a driver and a drummer. He became an assistant stage manager and took to the stage inspired by the stars of the old music hall. He changed his name to Benny after the American comedian, Jack Benny. He started slowly touring working men's clubs, small theatres and night clubs. After the war, he worked as a radio performer. His first tv role was in 1949 in a programme called, 'Hi there!' His career took off in 1955 when the BBC gave him his own show, 'The Benny Hill Show.' The show ran with the BBC until 1968. During that time, Benny also did work for ATV. In 1969, the Benny Hill show moved to Thames Television until 1989 when, due to political correctness and the distain of comedians such as Ben Elton, the show was cancelled. Benny had been a huge star and had a number one hit, 'Ernie' in 1971. When the show was cancelled, Benny was forgotten by the tv channels and his health deteriorated. He needed a triple heart bypass which he declined. He died on 19th April 1992 at his home in Teddington. He was 68.

# More Laurel and Hardy

After their British tour, and after their visit to Plymouth where Ollie was taken ill, Laurel and Hardy travelled back to America on the 3rd June 1954 on the Danish ship, 'Manchuria'.
This photo shows a recovered Ollie on the left with Stan on the right. They're dining at the Captain's table.
Unfortunately, Ollie died three years later on the 7th August 1957. He was 65 years old.
Stan wrote about their journey back home, in a letter;
'We sailed from Hull, England on June 3rd on a Danish Cargo ship. The

voyage took 23 days, stopped in at St. Thomas (the Virgin Islands), Curaco Christobal and through the Panama Canal. It was very interesting, especially the Canal. The accommodations were very nice - good food and calm sea all the way, I really prefer travelling this way as you don't have to dress up for meals etc as you do on the big passenger ships. There were only 10 passengers on this trip (12 is the limit they carry) so its practically like being on a private yacht.'

Stan died on the 23rd February 1965 at his home in Santa Monica. He was 74.

# Houdini Centenary

August 2009 marked 100 years since Harry Houdini jumped off the Stonehouse Bridge. The event took place on August 18th, 1909. Unfortunately, there seems to be no photos of the event or any of his appearance in the town or within the Palace Theatre. The Western Morning News covered the jump and it is probable that photos were taken at the time, however, many photos were lost and destroyed during the Blitz of 1941 and perhaps these were amongst them. If anyone knows of any photos of his visit to Plymouth, I'd love to hear about them.

Between 1900 and 1914, Houdini played at over a hundred venues within the UK. Houdini was a very generous man, When he performed his show in Edinburgh, he noticed how many children were without shoes. He performed a special show for the Scottish youngsters and made sure there were three hundred pairs of shoes so none would go away bare foot. There wasn't nearly enough shoes for the children that turned up so Houdini took them all to the nearest cobbler and made sure that everyone received a pair.

His appearance in Plymouth must have drawn huge crowds also. In a time when television was non-existent, someone like Houdini must have attracted people in their thousands.

It's amazing to think how Plymouth, and the world, has changed over the last 100 years. It's amazing that the Palace Theatre still stands although Stonehouse Bridge has seen many changes as well as being bombed in the Second World War.

Houdini went on to perform many more shows after he left Plymouth and he died on October 31st, 1926, aged 52.

# Cora Pearl

Cora Pearl was said to have been born in Caroline Place, Stonehouse on 23rd February, 1842. However, it is believed that she forged her birth certificate and was actually born in London in 1835. Her family moved to Plymouth in 1837.

She was born Emma Elizabeth Crouch and became a famous courtesan of the French demimonde in the 19th century.

Pearl had inherited her musical talent from her father, Frederick Nicholas Crouch, a composer and cellist. In 1867, she appeared in the role of Cupid in a production of Jacques Offenbach's, 'Orpheus in the Underworld.'

While working in London, she became involved in prostitution and had dalliances with several wealthy men. She became the mistress of Robert Bignell who owned the Argyll Rooms in Regent Street. Together, they travelled to Paris where she first adopted the name, Cora Pearl. She so

fell in love with Paris that she refused to return to London with Bignell. Pearl began a theatrical career there but was more known for her sexual appeal than her acting talents. Her theatrical reputation grew and she was soon linked with several wealthy men including the Duke of Rivoli. While she was with him, she developed a serious gambling habit and Rivoli, tired of bailing her out, eventually ended their affair.
She soon attracted other rich and powerful men who also became her benefactors.

A skilled craftsman could earn between two or four francs a day, whereas Cora earned 5,000 a night. She was famous for dancing nude on a carpet of orchards and bathing before guests in a silver tub of champagne.

The Duke of Grammont-Caderousse said at the time, 'If the Freres Provencaux served an omelette with diamonds in it, Cora would be there every night.'

Her lovers included Prince Willem of Orange, Prince Achille Murat and the Duke of Morny. Morny was Napoleon III's half-brother. Being financially sound, she rented Chateau de Beausejour in 1864, which lay on the banks of the Loiret outside Orleans.

When Morny died in 1865, Cora became the mistress of Prince Napoleon who was the cousin of Emperor Napoleon III. He purchased two home in Paris for her and also supported her financially until 1874. Although her activities made her very wealthy, her downfall resulted from her compulsive gambling and ultimately, her age. One story though seems to have led more to her downfall than others. She was the mistress of the wealthy Alexandre Duval who lavished her with gifts and money. When she chose to end the affair, Duval was so distraught that he shot himself on her doorstep. Rather than call for assistance or help him, she went back inside and went to bed. Duval survived but stories of the incident spread quickly and brought her theatrical career to a halt. She fled back to London but her popularity had waned and she eventually returned to Paris. With no benefactor to support her, she had to sell her possessions to support herself. In 1886, she became ill with intestinal cancer and had to move to a shabby boarding house where she died in poverty and was forgotten by most.

# Lillie Langtry

Lillie Langtry appeared at The Palace Theatre in Union Street in a production of 'The Crossways' on the 9th December, 1902. She played Virginia, Duchess of Keensbury in the production. Lillie Langtry was born Emilie Charlotte Le Breton in Jersey on the 13th October, 1853. She became a highly successful actress and was the mistress of King Edward VII. In 1874, Lillie married an Irish landowner called Edward Langtry. One of the attractions was that he owned a yacht and she insisted that he take her away from Jersey in it. They eventually settled in Belgravia in London. She became the subject of sketches and paintings after her appearances in London Society and through this she soon became quite well-known. She was nicknamed, 'Jersey Lily' because of her beauty. Her new found fame soon reached the attention of the Prince of Wales and after attending one of his dinner parties, she soon became his mistress. The affair lasted between 1877 and 1880. By 1879, Langtry had commenced an affair with the Earl of Shrewsbury and her husband announced that he would divorce her. Without her Royal connections, the Langtrys soon found themselves short of cash and realised that they

had been living a lifestyle beyond their means. In October 1880, many of their possessions were sold off to meet debts. Langtry also had many other publicised affairs. In 1881, she made her acting debut in 'She Stoops to Conquer' at the Haymarket Theatre in London. Oscar Wilde, a close friend, had suggested that she take up acting. She later became the mistress of two millionaires and eventually took up American citizenship. She died in Monaco on the 12th February, 1929, aged 75.

# H Leslie's Gay Lieutenants

I recently bought this rare postcard off ebay for just 99p! Amazingly, the picture was taken in September, 1909 so it's just over 100 years old. The photo features H Leslie's Gay Lieutenants and the picture was taken on Plymouth Pier. Although little is known about the group, they were probably a theatrical troop and would maybe have made appearances at other venues within the town. Their names are written in ink on the photo and these include Jack Willcox, Walter Banett, Fred Shephard, Jack Waller, Ella Elgar and Cecilia Gold. A note on the back of the postcard reads, 'Jack Waller married Cecilia Gold in 1910.'

H Leslie appears in theatre history and the earliest reference I can find of him is a playbill announcing a performance of 'H Leslie's celebrated London company, in The Princess of Trebizonde, at the New Theatre Royal, Park Row, Bristol, 18 September 1871.' He is billed as an orchestra leader which would suggest that the Gay Lieutenants were a musical troop. Other references show that H Leslie wrote songs with a fellow composer, G A MacFarren. One of the songs that Leslie wrote in the 1800s was, 'Speed on, my bark, speed on!' with an M Dee. At the same time, there is a composer mentioned called Henry Leslie and this is probably the same person. He is also listed as Henry T Leslie.

Of the troop, only Fred Shephard and Jack Waller's names appear in later productions. Jack Waller went on to compose songs for music hall and to put on stage shows with his business partner, Herbert Clayton. These included, 'Good News' in 1929 and 'Tell her the Truth', in 1933 which featured music by Waller. The partnership of Clayton and Waller was still producing stage shows as late as 1964, although it's hard to tell if they were both still alive then. Waller wrote many songs for shows including, 'Got the Bench, Got the Park', 'Roll Away Clouds' and 'Babying You' with his writing partner, Joseph Tunbridge. Shows that they wrote music for included, 'Silver Wings', Yes, Madam' and 'Princess Charming', all now long forgotten. Waller and Tunbridge would have been very well known in their day.

Fred Shephard wrote, 'Have we got the wind up, no not likely', another song that has long been forgotten.

It's amazing how much has changed in the 100 years since this photo was taken and anyone turning up to see a show called the Gay Lieutenants today would probably expect to see a whole different sort of act!

# Smeaton's Tower

Smeaton's Tower was built by John Smeaton on the Eddystone Reef in 1759. There had been two previous lighthouses in the same location. The first was built by Henry Winstanley in 1695. Unfortunately, seven years later, during a storm, it was washed away taking its builder with it.
The second lighthouse was built in 1711 by John Rudyerd but it was

destroyed by a fire in 1755. Work commenced on Smeaton's Tower in December 1756 to replace the damaged lighthouse. Smeaton's Tower would still be there today but the rock underneath it was undermined by the sea. James Douglass built a new lighthouse on an adjoining rock. It was felt that if Smeaton's Tower was left standing beside the new lighthouse, that it could eventually collapse onto the new lighthouse if the rock beneath it became even more undermined. It was decided to blow it up but a Mr F J Webb suggested that it should be dismantled and erected on the Hoe where the Trinity House Navigational Obelisk once stood. This was quite a task and the lighthouse was removed stone by stone and rebuilt on the Hoe with a new base to support it. The original base can still be seen beside the present Eddystone Lighthouse.

On 24th September, 1884, the Lord Mayor opened Smeaton's Tower on the Hoe to the public.

# A Tram at Saltash Passage

This very rare photo shows a tram at Saltash Passage in 1929. To the right of the tram, is the Royal Albert Bridge Inn and the building on the left is now a cafe.

The foreshore has now completely changed and nowadays, the area to the left in taken up by a small park which was built in the 1950s.

It's interesting to see the lack of traffic. There would have been few cars in the towns of Plymouth, Stonehouse and Devonport at the time and there was probably none at all in Saltash Passage. It's also interesting to see the tramlines which still lie there today underneath the modern tarmac.

The tram's destination is 'theatre' which referred to the termination point at Derry's Clock near to the old Theatre Royal. This is tram number 148 which had the longest route in Plymouth. At the time, trams would have brought many visitors to the nearby Little Ash Tea Gardens, the annual regatta and the St Budeaux Carnival.

The area by the cafe is where the American soldiers left for D-Day in 1944.

Saltash Passage has certainly seen some changes over the years but is still instantly recognisable from this old photo although one thing is noticeable - it was a far quieter place!

# The State Cinema

I pass the State Cinema in Victoria Road, St Budeaux, nearly every day. Of course, it's a long time since it's had that name. I read recently that there are plans to demolish it which I think would be a great shame.

In March 1939, just before the start of the Second World War, the St Budeaux cinema company was formed. They had a capital of £10,000 which was all in £1 shares. Perhaps if the cinema had been proposed further into the war, it might not have been built due to the lack of materials and resources.

On 16th October, 1939, a month into the war, the State Cinema opened at the junction of Victoria Road and Stirling Road. It seated 1,000 people and was the first cinema in Plymouth to be fitted with a four channel stereophonic system.

The first film shown was 'That Certain Age' starring Deanna Durbin and Melvyn Douglas. The seats were 6d, one shilling and 1/6d. There were two shows daily. The cinema was certainly popular and attracted huge queues whenever a new film was showing. It escaped the bombing during the war and stayed open for many years after.

I can remember in the late 1960s, queuing with my mother and brother to see films like 'Oliver' and 'Chitty Chitty Bang Bang'. I particularly remember queueing for Oliver because it was pouring down with rain and the queue went right around the building. I remember one evening, our parents took us there to see 'Ice Station Zebra' probably one of the most boring films I've ever seen!

In 1970, the name of the cinema was changed to the Mayflower to

coincide with the Mayflower celebrations of that year.

Eventually, the popularity of the cinema seemed to die off with the introduction of the video recorder. The Mayflower closed its doors to the film going public in 1983 and it became a carpet warehouse and, some time later, a snooker hall.

Once the cinema closed, the building was never kept in a particularly good condition and seems to have deteriorated ever since. Today, it stands boarded up with many of the younger generation not even realising it was once ever a cinema. It would be a great shame to see it go and hopefully, someone will decide to preserve it.

# Dad's Army

Remember the 1970s when there was actually something decent to watch on the telly? We all used to love Dad's Army then and it seems to have been repeated ever since!

I was reading the other day about Arnold Ridley who played Private Godfrey in the show. In Dad's Army, Godrey's character was that of a

former conscientious objector but in real life, Ridley fought as a Lance Corporal with the 6th Somerset Light Infantry during the First World War. When war broke out in August 1914, Ridley wanted to enlist straightaway but he was rejected because of a broken toe injury that he had endured while playing rugby. The following year, he tried to enlist again and was accepted and was sent, with other raw recruits, to train at Crownhill in Plymouth. The regimental Sergeant Major told them that they would not be seeing their families for a while because, 'you will all be bleeding well dead on the Western Front!'

Ridley was lucky to survive the battlefields of the Somme after being rescued by a fellow soldier who was later killed himself. In later life, he had nightmares and suffered terrifying flashbacks.

After the war, Ridley became a successful playwright but then experienced financial ruin until he regained fame in the classic sitcom. Arthur Ridley's story made me think about the real Dad's Army who protected Plymouth in the Second World War. The Home Guard, originally called the Local Defence Volunteers or LDV, was made up of members of the public who were told by Anthony Eden and his government to register, if they were interested in joining the LDV, with their local police station and when they were needed, they would be called up. Police stations found themselves deluged with volunteers and in just 24 hours, 250,000 people from all over Britain had registered their names. Although the age limit was supposed to be 65, many older members, some in there 80s, managed to enrol. Numbers grew and eventually one and a half million people registered their names.

Eden promised them all uniforms and weapons but they ended up with armbands and had to use whatever they could as weapons. These included pitchforks, brooms, umbrellas. golf clubs, pikes and catapults. Eventually, they were fitted out with denim uniforms and some rifles arrived.

Churchill changed the name of the LDV to the Home Guard in 1940 and he saw that they received proper military training. The Home Guard contributed to civil defence by helping to put out fires, clearing rubble, guarding damaged banks and shops and preventing looting. They also captured stray German parachutists and showed that they were ready to fight the enemy if they ever landed on British soil.

By 1943, the fear of German invasion was fading and the Home Guard found that they had lost most of their purpose in the War and numbers started dwindling.

In October 1944, the government announced that the Home Guard would be disbanded in the next month. There were no medals awarded and in total, 1,206 members of the Home Guard had either been killed on duty or died from their wounds and 557 more sustained serious injuries.

In December 1944, King George VI, the Home Guard's Colonel-in-Chief, stated, 'History will say that your share in the greatest of all our struggles for freedom was a vitally important one.'

# Memories of the US Army in Saltash Passage, 1944

I was lucky to know Marshall Ware, the St Budeaux historian, and I have many of his cuttings and notes amongst my collection. Marshall wrote down many things that happened in the Second World War and some of his reminisces I've included in my book, 'Memories of St Budeaux.'

When the American troops took over Saltash Passage in preparation for D-Day in 1944, everyone was issued with special passes so that they could enter the area. Marshall remembered, 'We all had identity cards but Saltash Passage residents were issued with yellow Certificate of Residence Cards. It bore the holder's National Registration Identity Card number and stated that the holder was thereby certified to be a resident within the specified area and that it must be carried out of doors at all times and shown to any Constable or member of His Majesty's or Allied Forces on duty. It bore the signature of the holder and was signed by the Chief Constable of Plymouth and the distribution was completed by 19th

## CERTIFICATE OF RESIDENCE

Serial No. *A705*

**FOR PERSONS WHOSE IDENTITY CARDS BEAR AN ADDRESS WITHIN THE AREA.**

1. M*rs Dorothy* HANCOCK (name)

of *1 Anemone Bungalow*

*Saltash Passage.* (address)

whose National Registration Identity Card No. is

*WEVT/11 19/3.*

is hereby certified to be a resident within the area specified in the Schedule to Direction No. under Defence Regulation 18A by the General Officer Commanding-in-Chief, Southern Command.

**VALIDITY :—UNTIL FURTHER NOTICE provided the place of residence remains unchanged. This certificate MUST be surrendered in the event of a change of address.**

2. This certificate must be carried out of doors at all times and shown on demand together with the holder's Identity Card to any Constable or member of His Majesty's or Allied Forces on duty.

Signature of holder *Dorothy Hancock*

*L.S. Parker* D.S.

For the Chief Constable of City *Plymouth SPECIAL BRANCH*

Date *19th April 1944*

S.C.P. 104. 1,200 pads of 100 (S/R 5537-9) 8-44

April 1944. One resident, wearing tennis gear, forgot to carry his card and was taken in a jeep for interrogation to the US Naval Advanced Amphibious Base at Vicarage Receiving Barracks at St Budeaux.'
The troops were very friendly and polite to the local residents and were loved by the children because they would give them sweets, gum, cocoa and other items that were rationed to the English. The Americans didn't have their food and supplies rationed at the time and were happy to share it with the locals.
Maurice Dart recalled, 'I remember the American's camp at Vicarage Road. When I was a boy, we would go down to the gate sometimes and they would give us chocolates and sweets and items to take home, such as tins of cocoa, biscuits and butter. My mother used to tell me off for scrounging but she was pleased to receive it all!'
This rare photo shows the smiling faces of the American troops as

they left for D-Day. Residents remember that the area was a hive of activity while the troops were there but, one day, they awoke to find that they'd all gone, leaving just a baseball bat behind.

# The Hoe Lodge Gardens, 1930s

This photo of the Hoe Lodge Gardens in the 1930s is an old picture used by the Keystone Press Agency. A quick search on the internet shows that Keystone are still in business.

Looking at this photo, not a great deal has changed over the years and the only noticeable thing that is now missing is the old bandstand which was dismantled in the 1940s during the Second World War.

This picture would have been featured in a newspaper or magazine at one time although it's impossible to discover what the story behind it was. This is possibly the only copy of this picture that survives. There is some information written on the back in pencil which reads, 'A pretty scene of the flower gardens on Plymouth Hoe. In the background can be seen Smeaton's Lighthouse.'

It must be Spring as one of the two girls in the picture is admiring the tulips while the other girl is holding an umbrella. In the background, Smeaton's Tower is painted as it is today though it's seen some variations over the years including being painted green and white during the 1960s. These were not only the colours of Plymouth Argyle but also the colours of Devon.

Also, in the background, can be seen the Victorian Watchtower which still stands today.

The garden had a small pond in the days before the Prejoma Clock. The clock was erected in April 1965 in memory of the parents of a Mr John Preston Ball.

It's amazing that this photo was taken over 70 years ago and it's incredible how little has changed over the years. Incidentally, this photo was another 99p buy on ebay. An absolute bargain, I think!

# Jack Waller

After my blog entry in September about H Leslie's Gay Lieutenants, who appeared on Plymouth Pier in 1909, I heard from Susan Allgaier in Wixom, Michigan who wrote:

'I live in Michigan and work with people who have Alzheimer's. One of my patients is the nephew of Jack Waller. Reggie's wife brought in an old scrapbook today with newspaper clippings and pictures of Jack Waller. How interesting! I hope to hear from you. Susan -Wixom, MI.'

I was amazed to hear from anyone who knew of, or remembered, Jack Waller and his troupe as he hardly gets any mention on the internet. It was lovely to correspond with Susan and to hear from Jack's great niece, Linda Margolin. Linda's memories of Jack certainly make interesting reading and give an insight to his personality, character and way of life. I've reproduced Linda's email below:

'Dear Derek,

I am Reggie's daughter and remember Uncle Jack well. I used to visit him whenever I returned to England. It was always exciting as they were 'different' than the rest of the family. Very posh. He was always dapper, with a cigar in his mouth and wearing beautiful clothes. Jack played the violin and used to soft-shoe dance down the corridor of the flat in Queen's Gate. He and his wife, my great-aunt Cecelia (my grandmother's sister) also had a fabulous "cottage" called Nanette (for obvious reasons) on the coast. I am having a senior moment trying to recall the exact town. They later moved to a huge gorgeous flat in St Johns Wood. After Jack died, Celia lived there with her sister Sylvia and the maid, Lizzie. Jack's portrait in oil, with cigar, always lived over the lounge fireplace with a special spotlight on it. Celia and Jack called each other mummy and daddy, and so daily Celia would talk to Daddy and tell him the news. After Celia died, Sylvia continued to live in St Johns Wood. When she died, as my dad and I were two of the heirs, I went to London to help sort things out. I have many old pictures of the two of them. I will try to get my scanner working again so I can send some to you. There is also a funny cookery book with favourite recipes of the Famous. Jack has one in there (Lizzie got NO credit!).We will be celebrating my Dad's 92nd birthday this Sunday at sunrise. I will tell him again of your interest in Jack. He will be pleased. Please keep in touch, I'd love to hear about your project. And perhaps there is more info I can give you. My husband and I hope to come to England next year, and we always go to Bournemouth as well to see my aunt and uncle. They also have great stories about Jack. Hope you are well. I am so glad Susan told me of her interest, and yours, in Jack.'

# Christmas during the Air Raids

In the 1955 copy of 'Christmas Cheer', Pat Twyford writes about
Plymouth and the Christmases during the Second World War. Some
people may have read Pat's diary that he kept during the war which was
called 'It Came to Our Door'. Henry Patrick Twyford was born in 1892 and
joined the Western Morning News in 1910 as a junior reporter. He fought
in the First World War but was invalided out in 1918 after being wounded
and gassed in the trenches. He rejoined the Western Morning News and
specialised in articles about football and agriculture. He became the
newspaper's war correspondent during the Second World War. He was
also a special constable and a member of the Seven

O' Clock Regulars, who regularly swam off the Hoe.

He was very interested in local history and compiled his book, 'It Came to our Door' in the years shortly after the war. He died in 1964.

His article in the Christmas Cheer magazine of 1955 mentions each year during the bombing of Plymouth. It begins,

'The approach of the 1939 Christmas was heralded with the distant rumble of war guns. Hearts were heavy. The war clouds hung dark and menacing. Would it all be over by Christmas? We hoped and we prayed but how fearful we were. Yet, even in our most anxious moments, we little realised how grim would be the Christmases of the next few years, what ordeals and sorrows we would have to endure before we could again capture the real spirit of Peace on Earth, goodwill towards men.'

When Christmas 1940 came, people tried to keep their spirits up but times were difficult with shortages of nearly everything that went to make a good Christmas. The celebrations and presents had to be planned far in advance as people did their best to get what they could. The Christmas bells remained silent and brightly lit shops and jostling crowds became just a memory. There were no Christmas trees with brightly coloured lights and tinsel and all the streets were dark and dreary with homes darkened by heavily blacked out curtains. Something that grew out of this was that people learned to live closer and draw strength from one another and also learned to share what little they had.

No-one could have predicted the devastation that came the following year. Christmas in 1941 followed a trail of destruction which destroyed much of Plymouth and many people lost their lives.

Pat Twyford remembered,

'It was indeed with a heavy heart that we approached the 1941 Christmas. Yet, my memory tells me, that there was still shining through the smoke and rubble of a distraught devastated city, the spirit of enduring courage, the will to make the best of things, to carry on as individuals and a community drawn together by tragedy. There was the simple roughly painted board over the north porch of the destroyed mother church of St Andrew, bearing the single word, 'Resurgam', which was an inspiration in Plymouth's agony.'

The Western Morning News of 1941 described the Christmas as 'a revelation of enterprise and improvisation, and above all things the abiding qualities of the people.'

There were now many people missing at family gatherings. These included people who were away fighting, children who had been evacuated and people who had unfortunately been killed during the Blitz. Carols were sung in darkened streets and collections were taken to aid welfare and relief funds. There were visits to the hospitals by civic heads and crowded services in many churches. Amazingly, a pantomime was performed at the Palace Theatre, 'Robinson Crusoe', which lifted many people's spirits. It was a make-do Christmas and the shortages were acute and rabbit featured on many a Christmas menu. It was still a Christmas that mothers made memorable for their children using courage, ingenuity and sacrifice. Old and discarded toys were rescued from cupboards and redistributed to children less fortunate. People opened their doors to service men and women so that they could share their Christmas. Carols were sang and everyone tried to keep up their spirits even though devastation lay all around them.

There were many more hardships to be endured in the Christmases of the next few years even after the end of the war in 1945.

Pat Twyford concluded in 1955, 'the lights have long since gone up in our streets and shops, out of the ashes of the old Plymouth, the new Plymouth has arisen. The bells ring out their message again with increased meaning, the good things are back for all to enjoy.'

Perhaps with all the hardships of a Christmas during the war, the thing that kept it all together was the generosity of friends, neighbours and strangers and everyone making do and sharing what they could.

# Christmas Cheer

Here's a picture of the cover of the 1955 copy of Christmas Cheer. The picture shows children having a snowball fight by Drake's statue on the Hoe.

The booklet was 64 pages long and featured some interesting stories including tales of the Old Stoke Gibbet, Plymouth in 1855, Disaster in the Sound, Christmas in the Air Raids, the Story of Gogmagog, an article about the old people of Plymouth as well as plenty of Christmas quizzes and the odd ghost story.

The tale of the Stoke gibbet is a dark and macabre one. It is a true story that tells of the murder of a dockyard clerk on the night of July 21st, 1787. Philip Smith was brutally bludgeoned to death near to Stoke Church. His murderer, a John Richards, together with an accomplice, William Smith, were both soon apprehended. Richards was a dock worker who had earlier been suspected of killing a Fore Street sentinel. At first, there were no clues to who had committed the crime but Richards soon boasted of the crime and was, shortly afterwards, arrested. However, there was little evidence against him and he was soon released. A hat found beside the body was identified as belonging to

Richards accomplice, William Smith. Hearing of this, Smith fled to Dartmouth but was soon caught and admitted to his role in the murder and implicated Richards. Both men were tried for murder at Heavitree. They were found guilty and condemned to death and executed in 1788.

The judge in the case, Judge Buller, declared that their bodies wouldn't by given to surgeons for dissection, which was usually the case, but were to be 'suspended between Heaven and Earth as they were fit for neither.' The corpses were brought from Exeter to Stoke and displayed near the scene of the crime. This gruesome practice was common at the time.

The bodies were hoisted in wire cages and chains on a gibbet erected on the muddy Deadlake beach just below Stoke Church. Smith's body stayed there for seven years before the gibbet collapsed and Richards' body stayed there slightly longer.

People avoided the spot and it was said to be 'the terror of some and the disgust of many'. Nettleton's 'Stranger's Guide to Plymouth' says that the gibbet stood in place upwards of 38 years near the Mill-bridge until it was blown down in the gale of 1827.

In 1788, a bestseller called, 'The Genuine Account of the Trial of Richards and Smith' sold 25,000 copies. Some were sold around the base of the gibbet.

Long after the gibbet disappeared, people shunned the area after dark which, during the 1830s, left the area quiet enough for grave robbers to carry out their grim practices in the secluded Stoke churchyard.

# Kinterbury Villa

This old postcard from 1923 is probably the only photo of Kinterbury Villa, who played against local teams and hailed from St Budeaux. They were the winners of the Junior League Cup in that year. When the team disbanded in 1924, some players left to join other teams including the popular nearby team, the Saltash Stars. Football was as popular then as it is now and there were many local teams including Woodland Villa who were great rivals of the St Budeaux teams from 1918 onwards.

Most of the names of the players have long since been forgotten although two members of the team at the time were Bob Foster and Reuben Woolway. Bob, who played inside left, left the team to join the Saltash Stars and later played for Cornwall. Reuben was the team's goal keeper and later joined Looe FC.

# The Forum
# in Devonport

Passing the Forum in Devonport today, it's hard to imagine that it once formed part of the busy and popular Fore Street. The heavy bombing during the Second World War, and the demolition afterwards, has left the now bingo hall almost on an island with constant traffic passing by all day long.

The Forum was once a popular and busy picture house. The cinema, which seated 1,800, opened on the 5th August, 1939. It's first film was 'Honolulu', which was shown at 5pm, which starred Robert Young and Eleanor Powell.

It was built by Charles Tyler of Swansea and was run in conjunction with the nearby Hippodrome.

Due to the heavy bombing in the war, Fore Street was partly cleared away and taken over by the dockyard and the cinema was never fully restored to its former glory. Television also played a part in dwindling audiences. The cinema stayed open until 14th May, 1960 and soon after, it opened as a bingo hall. Bingo seemed to lose favour for a while but now appears to be as popular as ever.

This photo shows the bomb damaged Forum and the destroyed shops of Fore Street beside it leading down towards the dockyard.

# Wembury Point Holiday Camp, 1930s

Many people who go for a walk at Wembury Point will know that the area once incorporated HMS Cambridge but perhaps they won't know what the area was used for in the 1930s. There are clues to be found on the foreshore including the remains of an old swimming pool.

Before the Second World War, the area was the location of a busy and

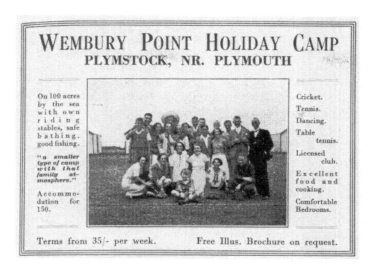

WEMBURY POINT HOLIDAY CAMP
PLYMSTOCK, NR. PLYMOUTH

On 100 acres by the sea with own riding stables, safe bathing, good fishing.

"a smaller type of camp with that family at- mosphere."

Accommo- dation for 150.

Cricket.
Tennis.
Dancing.
Table tennis.
Licensed club.
Excellent food and cooking.
Comfortable Bedrooms.

Terms from 35/- per week.    Free Illus. Brochure on request.

very popular holiday camp. The Southern Railway Handbook of 1936 carried an advert for the camp at Wembury Point. It was described as, 'a smaller type camp with that family holiday atmosphere'. The camp boasted that it featured a licensed club, excellent food and cooking and comfortable bedrooms. Pastimes included cricket, tennis, dancing and table tennis. The advert also stated that the camp was, 'on 100 acres by the sea with its own riding stables, safe bathing and good fishing'. There was accommodation for 150 and the cost to stay started at 35 shillings a week.

It all seemed to come to an end at the beginning of the War. In 1940, a Gunnery Range was established at Wembury and the whole area was later acquired by the Navy in 1950.

The holiday camp and all the fun that was once had there, seems to be long forgotten but here are a couple of rare photos that show what the area was once like. Older residents of Plymouth may remember visiting the camp when they were children or will have photos of their parents having fun there. The photos featured here show an advert for the camp and a group photo taken in 1938. How times change!

# Tamerton Foliot

The history of Tamerton Foliot dates back hundreds of years and it's interesting how parts of it have changed little over the last century although there are many new buildings.

There doesn't seem to be many old photos of Tamerton Foliot so I thought that I would feature some here.

The first photo features the once very busy railway station. At one time, it was very popular and looks very well kept in this picture, complete with tidied lawn and Pampas Grass. The stationmaster and his wife, along with a porter, can be seen in this photo which dates from the early 1900s. The station has been disused for many years now but the station house and platform can still be found near the beginning of the nature reserve. Nowadays, it's been turned into a family dwelling.

The next photo is from the 1880s and shows Fore Street. The chapel is on the right. There is a lot of activity in the photo and many people seem

to have gathered to pose for the photographer. Wandering through Tamerton Foliot today, parts of it still have the feel of a village that hasn't changed in hundreds of years although this scene has certainly altered since this picture was taken.

The next photo was taken at the bottom of the village and features Tamar House, which was once a coaching inn, in the middle of the picture . To the left, is Island House. Some of these buildings have now gone although it's quite easy to work out from where this was taken.

The man with the cart is the local road sweeper, Jack Maker. This photo was taken in the 1920s. He kept the streets clean at Maristow, Bickleigh and Tamerton where he lived with his wife who was the cook at the local vicarage.

Finally, the football team shown is the Tamerton AFC Cup Winners. This photo is from the 1948/49 season. Included in this photo are R Smith, H Bryant, J Pedrick, W Reeves, G Copp, C Tutton, A Morgan, E Glasson, W Bryant, N Richards, R Rendle, H Hunt, A Cutler, A Short and M Mabin. The little boy is the team's mascot, Kenneth Glasson.

# The Obelisk at Mount Edgcumbe

There is a story that the Obelisk was erected to celebrate the life of the Countess of Mount Edgcumbe's pet pig, Cupid. However, other sources say that the Obelisk was erected, in its current position, by Timothy Brett in 1770 in honour of his friend, George, the 3rd Baron of Edgcumbe. Brett was a former Commissioner of the Navy.

The Obelisk was originally sited where the Folly now stands. The 50 ft monument has been used as a navigational point by various shipping in the Sound over the years.

As mentioned earlier, Cupid the pig was said to have been buried in a gold casket beneath the obelisk when he died in 1768. In the book, 'Animals Graves and Memorials' by Jan Toms (Shire Publications 2006), it says that when the obelisk was moved to its present position, in 1770, nothing was found. However, the date of 1770 may be misleading as the obelisk appears in its present position on shipping maps as early as 1768.

As this was the year that Cupid died, it might be reasonable to assume that he is buried beneath the obelisk in its present position.

It is known that Fern Dell once contained an urn that commemorated Cupid but this has since disappeared. However, it is also recorded that Cupid was buried at Fern Dell and this was noted by George III and Queen Charlotte.

The dates prove confusing. For instance, the Folly was said to be erected on the spot where the Obelisk originally stood. However, the folly was erected in 1747 so how could Cupid have died and been buried beneath the obelisk, in its original position, in 1768? Research shows that the obelisk in its original position had already collapsed when the work to build the folly got underway.

In ' A Complete Parochial History of the County', published in 1870, it states, 'In the Cypress Grove is a monument to the memory of Timothy Brett Esq, one of the commissioners of the Navy, who, about the year 1770 erected the obelisk on the knoll near Cremyll as a memorial for his regard of his friend, George, the 3rd Baron of Edgcumbe.'

At the time, George was still alive and serving in the Royal Navy. During 1770, he was promoted to Vice Admiral and was appointed Vice Treasurer of Ireland.

Today, the obelisk is almost hidden away on a hill behind the Mount Edgcumbe Arms. There is no plaque on the monument to say who it is dedicated to and it's probably seen better days. It's hard to imagine now that it once stood where the folly stands.

To add to the confusion, the date, '1st July,1867', has been carved into the base of the obelisk. Beside the date is the name, 'R F Crowther'.

This mystery has, however, since been solved. Richard Crowther was enrolled during the 1860s on the boys training ship, 'HMS Impregnable' which was moored off Cremyll. One day, Richard wandered towards the obelisk from the training ship armed with a hammer and chisel and left the inscription and date. He was born in 1853 so would have been 14 years old in 1867 when he left his mark.

Cupid's remains may or may not be buried beneath the Obelisk but please don't go looking for them! There is more information about the history of the Mount Edgcumbe estate in my book, Mount Edgcumbe (ISBN 9780956078117 published by Driftwood Coast 2009).

# The St Budeaux Carnival

Here's the front page of the Western Morning Mercury from Saturday, 9th August, 1919. I think this is probably the only copy of this that survives.
The front page carries the story of the St Budeaux Carnival and I feature parts of it in my book, 'Memories of St Budeaux'.
The caption underneath reads :
'The Peace Carnival held at Lower St Budeaux on Monday was a

splendid success and gave great enjoyment to thousands. Our photograph is that of some of those who took part in the day's proceedings and were attired in fancy dress'.

Also on the front page was a story carrying the headline, 'St Budeaux Sports'. It read:

'In the field attached to the Naval Camp at St Budeaux, the lower St Budeaux Peace Sports, which were interrupted on Monday by the bad weather, were continued on Wednesday evening.

The success which attended the celebrations on Bank Holiday Monday, marked the proceedings again yesterday, and taking into consideration the spontaneity of the whole affair, great credit is due to the organisers. Everything had been greatly facilitated by the kindly co-operation of Commander Armitage and the officers and ratings of the Naval Camp. P O Stout, as chairman of the Sports Committee, put in a great deal of hard work.

At the close, Commander Armitage distributed the prizes and a vote of thanks was passed by the committee to him and his understudies for all they had done for St Budeaux. Commander Armitage, in returning thanks, led cheers for the committee, who had 'done all the work'. After the sports, an al fresco entertainment was given by the 'Dons' Concert Party. Messrs Staddon Hancock (sports secretary), and Hare acted as starters. P O Stout (chairman of the Sports Committee) was clerk of the course.'

The article then gives the names of people who won various events. These included the 100 yards race, the egg and spoon race, catch-the-cockerel, the sack race, the obstacle race, field racing, the blindfold race, the wheelbarrow race, the potato race, thread-the-needle race, the skipping race, the girl's three-legged race, the veterans' race, the 100 yards ladies over 40 race and the committee race. The article also mentioned that in the tug-of-war for boys, the Weston Mill district beat the Saltash Passage district.

# Plymouth Hoe in the snow

With the recent snow downfalls, I thought that I would include a few photos of a snowy Plymouth Hoe.

The first photo shows the tree-lined walkway up to the Hoe. At one time, sheep were regularly grazed on the banks of the Hoe. Here, they're being tended to by their owners as they desperately search for grass to eat.

The second photo shows a Victorian snow scene. Smeaton's Tower can be seen in the background and much of the Hoe looks like it does today. The memorial at the bottom right of the picture has now long gone.

95

The third photo shows a Victorian lady making her way up from the Pier. The clock appears to read 7.50am. The tramlines can clearly be seen on the road and a horse and cart are approaching the Pier entrance. In the background can be seen the snow covered roofs at West Hoe. Elliot Terrace can also be seen on the right and a group of men have gathered above the Belvedere. Again, not much has changed in this scene.

The fourth photo dates from a later time and shows a man pulling his son on a sledge. In the background, three men are having a snowball fight. The snow all looks lovely to see and it makes for some great photos although I imagine that many of the people in these photos were glad to see the back of it. There would have been no central heating, cold weather payments or electricity in Victorian times and the cold weather probably meant misery to many.

# More photos from the St Budeaux Carnival, 1919

Here are two more photos of the St Budeaux Carnival from the Western Weekly Mercury of Saturday, 9th August, 1919.
The first photo shows the group of officials who organised the Carnival, which took place on the previous Monday. The picture shows two policemen, the ferryman, local businessmen and men and women from the community. There is also a schoolboy in the front row. Lots of fancy hats were worn by the women.
In the second picture, local people are dressed up for a procession through the town which, the paper states, caused roars of laughter from

the crowds that had gathered to see them. Amongst the group are several clowns, minstrels, pixies, farmers, a policeman, a brick layer, a cavalier, a labourer and a banjo player.

It looks like it was quite an event. I wish I had more photos from newspapers of the Carnival in following years but it seems that most have long since been thrown away.

There would have been a happier outlook to the Carnival of 1919 as the First World War would have recently ended although there would also have been much sadness at the loss of so many young men from the area.

The carnival of this year was also known as the Peace Carnival.

# The Great Blizzard of March 1891

With the heavy downfall of snow recently and with the whole country coming to a standstill, I thought that it would be good to write about one of the most remembered blizzards which devastated the area over 100 years ago.

The Great Blizzard of March 1891 affected many parts of the country particularly the South West. The strong gales and heavy snowfall hit

Cornwall, Devon, Dorset, Herefordshire and Kent. London was also hit by the strong winds and snowfalls.

The devastation left behind included uprooted trees and many fences and roofs were blown away also. The storms were so ferocious that much of Cornwall and Devon were cut off from the rest of Britain for four days between 9th and 13th March, 1891. In this time, over 200 people were killed as well as 6,000 animals.

At a time when there were no cars, no electricity, no televisions, few telephones and no wireless, the heavy downfall meant that you really were cut off from the rest of the country.

The Times in March 1891 stated that 'no such storm had visited the West of England within remembrance.'

Temperatures dropped below zero and snow drifted in places up to 15 feet high. A train heading from Yelverton towards Princetown was trapped by a large snowdrift and remained in place overnight. It's 3 crew and 6 passengers huddled in a carriage and were finally rescued by a local farmer tending to his sheep. The line remained shut for several weeks afterwards.

The photo shows a Victorian snowball fight on Plymouth Hoe. A boy hides behind the snowman to give the appearance that he too is throwing a snowball!

# German Prisoners of War at St Budeaux

The following rare photo, featured in a local newspaper during the early 1940s, shows captured German airmen helping to build pre-fabricated homes for the people of Plymouth.

In the background can be seen the church at Higher St Budeaux. Many people will remember the pre-fabs that stood in the area long after the war had finished. They were only built to last for ten years but most lasted much longer. Some can still be found at the nearby Ernesettle Lane.

There seems to be little mentioned about captured German prisoners of war within Plymouth and it seems ironic that the airmen were put to work building houses for the homeless when they would have caused the problem in the first place. They were known locally as 'Herrenvolk' which is a translation of 'The Master Race', which was probably applied to them sarcastically rather than with any respect. I can't find any reports of how they were treated, although they were probably treated well, but local people would have despised them as many would have lost their friends,

neighbours and families in the heavy German bombing particularly in 1941. Even so, local children would have been fascinated by them and probably pretended to machine-gun them every day on their way to school!

Higher St Budeaux still has a village feel about it in this picture with very few buildings and plenty of open land. On the left can be seen the St Budeaux Foundation School which was demolished when the new road and roundabout were put in place, in the early 1980s, which led to the Parkway. Also in the picture is Higher St Budeaux Church and the nearby Inn, remembered fondly as 'The Blue Monkey.'

A lot has changed over the years and it's strange to think that many of the roads and paths that are still in place were originally laid by German airmen.

# The Way We Live

There's an interesting film, called 'The Way We Live', which was shot in Plymouth in 1945. It stars Patsy Scantlebury as Alice Copperwheat whose family's house is destroyed in the Blitz and they're billeted at Horrabridge before moving into a newly built pre-fab.

The film starts with a writer, played by Peter Willes, travelling to Plymouth to see what the new plans for the rebuilding of the city involve. There is interesting footage showing Plymouth devastated. Only a few buildings remained complete in the city centre after the heavy bombing. Seeing it as moving footage somehow makes it all more real and it almost appears more recent than just looking at old photographs. There are clips of the Hoe which includes dancing on the Promenade and also

film of Efford, the Barbican, the railway station and many other areas around the city.

The film was financed by J Arthur Rank and was directed by Jill Craigie, who later became Mrs Michael Foot. A young Michael Foot appears in later parts of the film together with Sir Patrick Abercrombie, the architect of the new city, Winston Churchill, Lady Astor and James Paton Watson, the city engineer. Rank's accountant tried to halt the production of the film half way through because he felt that it wasn't commercial enough for general release. The film went ahead after Craigie appealed to Rank and trial runs were hosted at cinemas that were usually hostile to documentary films. The audience of one East End cinema booed it but after it was championed by a notable film critic, the film was released nationwide. Amazingly, it broke all box office records in Plymouth and one audience member said that it, 'revived the interest of the man in the street in what was to be done to erase the scar which lies across the city.' Watching the film today, it's hard to imagine that people were ever so posh. It's interesting to watch though to see how the city has changed over the last 65 years and I can see how people then would have been very impressed with the new city centre after the devastation of the old one.

Peter Willes, who played the writer in the film, went on to appear in bit parts in future movies before becoming a executive producer on many tv productions throughout the 1960s and 1970s. Many of the other actors in the film though were never heard of again.

Patsy Scantlebury, who lived in St Budeaux, was chosen for the role after being seen on Plymouth Hoe jitterbugging with an American sailor. At the time, she was just 17. She had previously worked in a post office. Patsy signed a seven year contract with Rank and played an air hostess in 'Blind Goddess' as Patsy Drake. There doesn't seem to be much information about her after this but today, she would be about 82.

# Elephants in Bedford Street

Here's a lovely photo taken in Bedford Street in the early 1900s. The circus was in town and its many elephants were paraded through the streets of Plymouth. The circus would have been a huge attraction back then and would be the only chance that people would have to see such wild animals so close up. A group of boys have gathered on the left of the picture and one of them is feeding one of the elephants. On the right, is a man on a chariot and on the left is what appears to be the ringmaster, complete with straw boater and whip. In the far background, is an ornately decorated float being driven by many finely dressed horses. On top of the float, almost twelve feet up, are characters from the forthcoming show complete in their elaborate costumes.

A parade through the streets like this would have assured that many people knew the circus was in town and would guarantee that children would pester their parents to take them to the show. In an age with no televisions or cinema, the only contact children would have had with animals such as tigers and elephants would be through books and comics. Being taken to the circus would have been an exciting and fascinating experience for them. Imagine the talk in the playground the next day. The same children might have also been to shows to see Houdini or Buffalo Bill who also appeared in Plymouth around about the same time.

It's an amazing animate scene and the once grand Globe Hotel can be seen in the background. Unfortunately, it's all now long gone. Bedford Street was destroyed in the Blitz of 1941 and a parade of elephants through the streets of Plymouth today would probably be frowned upon.

# Skull and Crossbones at Eggbuckland Cemetery

Anyone visiting the cemetery at St Edwards Church at Eggbuckland, and many other cemeteries around the country, might think that they've discovered the graves of pirates when they see the markings of the skull and crossbones on ancient headstones.

In Leixlip Church in County Kildare, the same skull and crossbones can be found and it is said that many members of the military are buried there from the time of the crusades. A stone at the southeast corner of the church bears a connection to the Knights Templar Crusaders with a worn symbol of the skull and crossbones.

However, the skull and crossbones in Eggbuckland cemetery neither marks the graves of members of the Knights Templar or pirates. Some people have suggested that the graves are the victims of plague or poisoning or that the people buried there were Catholics. The truth is, however, not so romantic. In the 1600s and 1700s, attitudes to death were very different to what they were in the 1800s and later.

The motifs were put there just as a reminder to the living of what happened to the bodies after death. People were judged on the lives they led and not on the hope of forgiveness in the afterlife.

# Plymouth's Volcano

With all the catastrophes around the world at the moment, it might surprise many people in Plymouth that they live so close to an extinct volcano. Looking around the city, it is probably, nowadays, almost impossible to guess where it is. Many people would probably look inwards towards the land in their search for it but you're more likely to guess its location by looking out towards the sea. From the Hoe, looking out towards the Sound, is a giant plug that seals off the vent of this once active volcano.

Have you guessed it yet? Yes, the plug I'm talking about is now Drake's Island.

The shores of Kingsand are made up of a purple volcanic rock called Rhyolite. A close inspection of the rock shows that some of it contains thousands of gas bubbles from the volcano's last eruption. Rhyolite is a rock formed by the solidification of molten magma. For all of you concerned about an imminent eruption, don't worry! The last eruption took place a very long time ago. The Rhyolite dates from the Permian Period (299 - 251 million years ago) which represents a geologic period which included the diversification of early amniotes into the predecessors of mammals, turtles, lepidosaurs and archosaurs. It is the last period of the Paleozoic Era and included the largest mass extinction known to science. Ninety percent of all marine species became extinct, as did seventy percent of all land organisms.

# Goulds in Ebrington Street

Here's a lovely old photo showing where Goulds Surplus Store stands today.

Frederick Gould founded the shop in the early 1900s and they had outlets in various parts of Plymouth before moving into their present building in 1955. Many older residents will remember that the building once housed the Cinedrome, a cinema that was bombed during the Second World War. It's unique facade still remains and Plymouth City Council are eager to retain the older parts of the street including the old shop fronts.

This photo features the number 24 tram on its route from Prince Rock to the Theatre Royal by Derry's Clock. With the constant heavy traffic nowadays, it's hard to imagine that trams ever travelled that way and were the main form of transport. It's a very quiet scene and the tram driver seems to have stopped to pose for the camera. The only person on board is the conductor who is right at the back.

There are many interesting adverts on the walls of the buildings including ones for Pophams, G P Skinner, H Matthews' Restaurant, Four Castles Tea and a production at the local theatre. I wonder how many of these names are remembered by the people of Plymouth today? Pophams survived to well after the war but, today, is now long gone.

I haven't been along Ebrington Street for a long time but this photo makes me want to go there again and see just how much has changed over the years.

# Tarmac

Driving around Plymouth today, you can't help but notice all the potholes everywhere. In many places, the old cobbled roads underneath the tarmac are being revealed. Saltash Passage is one particular place where the cobbles are appearing and it's easy to imagine what the area must have once looked like when trams travelled towards the ferry taking passengers over to Saltash.

Many people will think that tarmac is a relatively new thing but amazingly, tarred roads date back to the 8th century and appeared in Baghdad at the time.

Tarmac as we know it today has been around since 1903. Patented by Edgar Purnell Hooley in 1901, some of the streets of Plymouth were tarmaced in the early 1900s including roads in Stonehouse which were paid for by the then Earl of Mount Edgcumbe.

Previously, Macadam road surfaces were used from 1820 and invented by Scotsman, John Loudon MacAdam. He called the process, macadamisation.

McAdam's road surfaces were ideal for horses and carriages but were dusty and eroded when it rained. Once motor transport was introduced, the roads couldn't cope and a new formula containing tar was used.

Hooley's patent involved mechanically mixing tar and aggregate and this was prepared before it was put on the road surface and compressed using a steam roller.

Today, cobbled streets and lovely paved footpaths are regularly tarmaced over much to the annoyance of people who prefer the streets as they are, a reminder of times gone by. It's amazing to think that this whole process isn't a new one and has been going on in Plymouth for well over 100 years.

The photo shows Bedford Street on the day that the circus came to town. No cobbled streets there, just a dusty old macadam road.

# More about the Silver Mine of Saltash Passage

I've had a lot of people write to me recently about the underground mine at Saltash Passage and it all makes very interesting reading. With the work recently being carried out at the bottom of Little Ash Gardens to repair subsidence, together with past damage to the houses on the left-hand side of Little Ash Gardens, it's easy to follow the route of the final leg of the mine.

I had a very interesting letter from Terry (whose surname I unfortunately don't know) and I hope that he doesn't mind me reproducing it here as it sheds some light on the tunnel and the route it took.

Terry writes:
**'I was very interested to read , 'The Silver Mine in Saltash Passage' on your blog. I lived in St Budeaux some 40 years ago, near**

Kinterbury Creek. We all called it 'Mud Cott' although I don't know why.

What I now know as the silver mine, we called 'Smugglers Cave'. I used to go in often and I was one of the children they sealed it up to keep out!

In the mid 1960s, you could go in and just inside was a large boulder which you had to go around. After you got passed it, you were in a large chamber. There was a bench/bed carved out of rock. There was one main tunnel and the beginning of another but that was only a few feet in. The main one headed towards the main road. It must have been quite level because there was an inch or two of water along the bottom. As you went through, there were a few bends and at the end, it just got smaller and stopped. It didn't go in a very long way as I remember, under Little Ash Gardens at the most, so I would be very surprised if it went as far as Vicarage Gardens. I have for years wondered what it was. I assumed it was for the Home Guard to watch the river and bridge during the War. Maybe they did use it.

I still visit Plymouth and last year, I went to have a look. You can't see it now, there is a boat house or something in front.

Also, when I lived there, if you went along the beach on the opposite side to the mine side, where the cast iron pipes go into the river, there was a large sheet of twisted metal with rivet holes and rivets in. We used to try and move it when we were crabbing but it was

**stuck solid in the mud. It's not there now, perhaps it was taken away for scrap, and I wondered if it was part of the ammunition barge blown up in the War?'**

I enjoyed Terry's informative letter very much and I wish that I had his address but hopefully, he'll write again. I would also be very interested to hear from anyone else with tales of the area. They certainly make very interesting reading.

# Plymouth in the 1950s and 1960s

These few photos show Plymouth city centre during the late 1950s and early 1960s.

The first picture shows a very busy town centre. Many people will remember the streets crowded like this, before the area was pedestrianised. On the left can be seen the Dolcis shoe shop at 37 New George Street which adjoined Dingles. Further down can be seen the old Western Morning News building which today houses Waterstones. The fashions have certainly changed over the years. A lone sailor can be seen in the foreground in the days when wearing their uniform was compulsory. The now old fashioned cars, parked on the left, all look very much the same model and there certainly wasn't the choice there is nowadays. Most came in either black, grey or green. This was to become a far more busy scene in the 1970s and 1980s when every parking meter had a car beside it and in-town parking was almost impossible at busy times.

The second photo, from the same period, shows British Home Stores in Cornwall Street. The buildings haven't changed that much in the 50 or so years since but the cars and fashions have changed greatly. The streets all look much more narrow with the many vehicles parked there.

The third photo shows Frankfort Gate and, at first glance, it looks like not much has changed over the years.
Many of the shops have changed ownership many times but the market can still be seen clearly in the background. Earlier shops in the area

included the popular stamp shop (probably a dying hobby now), Bonus Books, the Camera Exchange and, further around on the main road, Jack Cohen's Joke Shop. The red phone box has long gone and a huge green pedestrian walkway has been built in the centre of this scene. It all looks very tidy when this photo was originally taken and quite empty. However, anyone visiting these three areas nowadays would probably notice quite a bit of difference.

# King Street

King Street ran from Cambridge Street to Stoke Road and Manor Street. There doesn't appear to be many photos of the King Street arch in existence but this is the best one I've found. This photo dates from the early 1960s and shows the arch which was just after 144 King Street, which can just be seen on the left of the photo. Number 144 housed Cole's grocery shop.

Perhaps one of the most remembered shops in King Street was Ivor Dewdney's pasty shop which was at number 2 and which opened in the 1930s.

The photo shows interesting adverts for both Ovaltine and the Co-op. In the early part of the last century, hawkers and entertainers gathered underneath the arch. One was a Mr Pratt who, with his monkey, Bruce, entertained passersby with his organ grinder. Bruce wore a red hat and jacket and was well known to the people living in the area. Mr Pratt, his wife and his monkey all lived in one tiny room in the street. Small audiences would gather to watch Bruce and would feed him chipped potatoes which were sold in the evening by Italians living in the area. By day, they would sell ice cream around the town from their small handcarts.

Another well known figure was a blind Cornish miner who sold boot and shoe laces which were draped from his left arm while, with his right hand, he would hold out a tin cup to collect money.

Many beer houses sprung up in the area during the 1850s including the Thistle Rose and Shamrock, the Hen and Chicken and the Botanic Garden which was near Flora Street Nursery. In the shadow of the railway embankment stood the Robert Burns, the Broad Gauge and the Tandem Inn.

As a barrel organ played, bruised fruit was sold at knock down prices and women gathered to attend late night auctions selling cheap cuts of meat. Chestnut sellers would also ply their trade from a warm fire and a man on stilts would tap on windows to announce forthcoming events such as the fair or the circus. Rabbit formed a staple part of people's diet and a rabbit catcher with four or five rabbits hanging from his arm would sell and skin the creatures on the spot.

It all seems a world away from the King Street of today. Torn apart in the Second World War, the area has seen a lot of changes and rebuilding. When the arch was pulled down in the 1970s, a major part of the street disappeared and the hawkers and entertainers from nearly 100 years previous, were soon forgotten.

# The War Effort

All over Plymouth, there are the signs of missing railings and other ornate metal work. During the Second World War, as part of the War effort, houses were stripped of their railings and other metal was collected by the Ministry of Salvage to be melted down and used for munitions . Over 1.5 million tonnes were collected and the whole operation boosted morale and brought people together. Any metal that could be taken was quickly removed including the bandstand on the Hoe. On the walls of many old houses in Plymouth, you can still see where the railings were hacksawed away. Even the Mount Edgcumbe Estate removed its railings to help the campaign. On the 12th January 1942, work started in the Mutley area to remove all unnecessary railings although some of the more ornate railings survived the exercise. However, many were removed and were never replaced.

The Women's Voluntary Service were responsible for organising salvage drives which not only included the removal of railings but also the collection of aluminium pots and pans, jelly moulds, kettles, paper and rubber and even artificial limbs.

Children were banded together to collect as much salvage as possible including small items such as bottle tops. Regular salvage drives were organised to help the war effort. Tin, rubber, iron, steel, paper, cooking fat and even silk stockings were all collected. A popular poster during the War read, 'Salvage saves Shipping'.

Saturday Scrap collections were organised and children would knock at doors asking for any spare metal. This included gates, saucepans, empty tins and anything that could be spared. Some councils awarded certificates to recognise the work done by children.

However, while people happily banded together to help the war effort and collected a great deal of scrap metal to provide extra guns, tanks and planes for the troops, the truth was somewhat different. Little or none of the metal collected was ever melted down and used for the war effort and most was just dumped soon after.

# A Devonport Tram

At first glance, it's hard to place where this lovely pre-war tram is passing in Plymouth. There are several clues though. By enlarging the photo, a street sign can be seen beside the front of the tram which says 'Chapel Street'. Also, in the background, can be seen the word 'piano' and I can recognise this as a shop belonging to Hocking's Pianos which stood beside the Forum Cinema (now the Mecca Bingo Hall). The Forum, which was in Fore Street at the end of Chapel Street, stands just to the left of Hocking's and the rest of Fore Street, with its wonderfully ornate buildings, continued until it met the dockyard gates. The Second World War not only devastated Fore Street but also Chapel Street and none of the buildings shown in this photo still stand. The Forum is still there, of course, but the rest of Fore Street including the Devonport Market were incorporated into the dockyard and have been unseen by civilians for many years. Recently, the area enclosed in the dockyard has been refurbished and building work still continues.

For comparison, I've taken a photo of how the area looks today. Just for good measure, I made sure I got a picture of the tram's future replacement! The Forum can be seen in the far background on the left and an Esso garage stands where all those lovely buildings used to stand.

114

Walking further down, I thought that I could see tramlines in a pothole in the road. A similar thing was reported in Saltash Passage recently.
It's amazing how it's all changed over the years.

# Putty Philpotts

This photo shows Putty Philpotts who, at one time, was quite a well-known figure in the city. He led the Plymouth, Stonehouse and Devonport Carnival, shown here in 1926, which raised money for the Royal Albert Hospital (later Devonport Hospital). He was known as a giant of a man although this referred to his generosity as well as his weight. He was an ex-Navy man and also an ex-publican and, at twenty stones, was once the heaviest man in the services. After leaving the Navy, he ran the Brunswick Hotel in Stonehouse and would entertain people by playing the banjo beside the log fire there. Stars from the Palace Theatre would come to watch and would join in with his many songs including, 'South of the Border down Stonehouse Bridge Way' which he adapted from the more well-known, 'South of the Border'.
During the Second World War, The Brunswick Hotel was destroyed by a land mine and Putty then became the landlord of a pub in Devonport which, by coincidence, was bombed on his very first night there. He

ended his days as the landlord of the No Place Inn at Eldad Hill.
In between running various pubs, Putty also appeared in concerts
performing his many songs which included, 'Figgy Pudding'.
The Plymouth, Stonehouse and Devonport Carnival lasted all week and
Putty was often the Carnival king. Regular events included fancy dress
competitions, parades and stalls. It is said that when he died, the pall
bearers had to be 'fortified at the local bar' before carrying out their bulky
task!

# By the same author :

St Budeaux
Derek Tait

## St Budeaux

A history of St Budeaux, Plymouth. Contains over 150 old photos and illustrations.
108 pages.
Price : £9.99.
ISBN-13: 978-0955427763.

Saltash Passage
Derek Tait

## Saltash Passage

A history of Saltash Passage, Plymouth. Contains over 140 old photos and illustrations.
104 pages.
Price : £9.99.
ISBN-13: 978-0955427732.

Plymouth Hoe
Derek Tait

## Plymouth Hoe

A history of Plymouth Hoe. Contains 172 old photos and illustrations.
128 pages.
Price : £9.99.
ISBN : 978-0-9554277-7-0.

Plymouth
at War
Derek Tait

## Plymouth at War

A history of Plymouth. Contains 200 old photos and illustrations.
130 pages.
Price : £9.99.
ISBN : 978-0955427787.

## Plymouth

A history of Plymouth. Contains 200 old photos and illustrations.
130 pages.
Price : £9.99.
ISBN : 978-0955427794.

## Saltash

A history of Saltash. Contains over 150 old photos and illustrations.
128 pages.
Price : £9.99.
ISBN : 978-0-9560781-0-0.

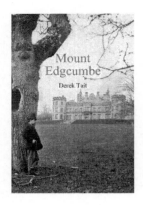

# Mount Edgcumbe

A history of Mount Edgcumbe. Contains over 203 old photos and illustrations.
172 pages.
Price : £9.99.
ISBN : 978-0-9560781-1-7.

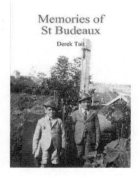

# Memories of St Budeaux

People's memories of St Budeaux. Contains over 111 old photos and illustrations.
104 pages.
Price : £9.99.
ISBN : 978-0-9560781-2-4.